# Personalized Whole Brain Integration

Published by
Edu-Kinesthetics, Inc.
Post Office Box 3395
Ventura, CA 93006-3395
U.S.A.
www.braingym.com

by Paul E. Dennison, PH.D.
& Gail E. Dennison

## The Basic II Manual on Educational Kinesiology

FOR YOUR INFORMATION

The procedures and techniques described in
this manual are solely for educational
purposes. The authors and Edu-Kinesthetics,
Inc., do not directly or indirectly present
any part of this work as a diagnosis or as a
prescription for any ailment for any reader or
student. Persons using the tests, procedures,
and corrections reported herein do so for
educational purposes only.

*"The teacher must heal, the healer must teach"*

# ACKNOWLEDGEMENTS

Our special gratitude to our personal teachers who have guided us toward this special work...

Also thanks to John F. Thie, D.C., Mary Marks, Gordon Stokes, Richard Harnack, Kim Viera and all the fine staff at the Touch For Health Foundation who believed in us when this work was only an idea...

Thanks also to our hundreds of students whose enthusiasm for E-K gave us the impetus to create this manual. Deserving special mention are Frank Mahony, Susan Kovarick, Wolfgang Gillessen, Joan Hulse, and Steve Rochlitz for recognizing the value in E-K and for sharing it selflessly with their friends.

Finally, a very special "thank you" to our first certified E-K instructor, Phillip Crockford, for introducing E-K around the world and to the school systems in the San Francisco area. His recognition of the importance of making E-K available to the classroom teacher and to people with little prior experience with holistic health motivated us to create courses and materials to meet these special needs. We thank Phillip, in addition, for his many suggestions for this manual and for the delightful names for the E-K Dimension Indicators.

# BASIC II TABLE OF CONTENTS

PREFACE
"Movement is Life"

Personalized Whole Brain Integration, the Basic II Class Manual
for Educational Kinesiology, is intended only as a supplement to
the information and "hands-on" experience of students who are
participating in the E-K II Workshop in Educational Kinesiology.
This workshop attracts teachers, parents, body workers, and pro-
fessionals who want to be more effective with people.  Educational
Kinesiology is a sound basis for all other therapies because it enables the student/client to integrate experiences with the whole
brain.

PERSONALIZED WHOLE BRAIN INTEGRATION:  THE WORKSHOP

This is the E-K class designed for people who have some background
in techniques of applied kinesiology, such as Touch for Health, or
who will be working on an individualized basis with students.  It
is also recommended that the student has experienced the "E-K for
Kids Workshop", which introduces the fundamentals of E-K with min-
imal muscle testing. This class will enable you to "switch on" to
a higher level of brain performance and a deeper appreciation of
your uniqueness through an understanding of your own hemispheric
dominance and how to maximize your innate potentials.

As in the "E-K for Kids Workshop", this "Basic II Workshop" emphasizes left brain/right brain integration.  The exercises begin
reeducating the body to function in the midfield where the two cerebral hemispheres must work together.  Students experience en-
hanced abilities in terms of visual and auditory perception and
general motor coordination.   Although it builds on the simple
group exercises offered in "E-K for Kids", it is more for those
one-on-one opportunities that allow for deeper and more permanent
change.

Although these processes have helped thousands to gain a greater
appreciation of life, these procedures have been found especially
successful in the repatterning of dyslexics and dysgraphics whose
lack of hemispheric integration makes learning difficult or impossible without this work.

1

# EDU-KINESTHETICS: THE ADVANCED E-K WORKSHOP

Edu-Kinesthetics means "education through movement". The "Advanced Edu-Kinesthetics Workshop" is a requirement for certification to be an E-K Instructor-Consultant and to teach the E-K basic workshops. The "Advanced Edu-Kinesthetics Workshop" addresses other levels of integration which build upon "E-K For Kids" and E-K II. The Edu-Kinesthetics Instructor has a broad set of tools to draw upon. He or she guides students towards a greater sense of themselves through new exercises with mind and movement. He sees each person's unique needs and unique ways of actualizing. He honors, supports and trusts the wisdom of that individual being's way of unfolding, rather than approaching him with any preconceived expectations about how he should evolve. A fuller experience of the Mind/Body System through Edu-Kinesthetics provides the participant with a foundation to meet life's challenges from a larger and more integrated sense of Self.


## A Special Note to the New E-K Student

In E-K, we use function-oriented language to describe the brain. For this reason, our synonyms for "left brain" and "right brain" may change, depending upon the tasks that we are discussing at the moment. Left/right and back/front brain neurology is far more involved than our model might suggest. Our purpose is not to understand the brain. Our purpose is to help people to better understand how to live their lives.

We use the brain descriptions found in this manual to establish a "language" with our "body" of knowledge. We can actually learn about our own preferred modes of functioning through this metaphor of brain-processes!

As teachers, writers, and artists, we use language to paint a picture, or to point to something that can be better understood with words and labels. However, our words are only an attempt to entice you into whole-brained movement. The whole-brain experience is elusive and must be experienced to be understood.

2

# ASSUMPTIONS

Educational Kinesiology is more than the muscle tests, procedures, and corrections which an observer might witness performed by the E-K consultant. E-K is a philosophy and point of view shared by those involved in this work. E-K is most successful for those who trust in these beliefs. A partial list of "assumptions" about liv‑ing, loving, and learning, held in common by E-K instructors is included here. How does your belief system compare to this list?

1. The natural state of the human being is the "integrated" state. This is the state of optimal health. Disease and "dys"abilities are survival mechanisms to adjust to the inability to achieve integration.

2. Human beings, if placed in a nurturing environment where their basic survival needs for food, clothing, shelter, and love are met, are naturally good.

3. Human beings are placed upon this planet to grow and change. Growth and change are inherent in man's nature.

4. Each human being is involved in the growth of every other human being with whom he comes into contact, for better or for worse.

5. Each human being must accept full responsibility for his inter-actions with every other human being on the planet.

6. Each human being creates his own reality and must accept total responsibility for his own life.

7. Members of the helping professions, in particular, must rec-ognize their responsibility to interact positively with their students and clients in a manner which heals, fosters change, and restores responsibility for growth to the individual.

8. Intention to nurture growth is the single most powerful tool in the healing arts. "Energy follows intention" and all who be-lieve in the above assumptions cannot fail to produce powerful, positive changes in their students.

9. Corrections must be specific. We cannot rely on growth changes to take place in a "general" way. Human beings do not always learn by transfer of learning from one area to the other.

10. Integration is never complete as long as there are new things to learn and new ways to grow.

E-K I:   E-K FOR KIDS WORKSHOP
Text:   <u>E-K For Kids</u> by Paul Dennison, Ph.D, and Gail Hargrove,
1985.   suggest  8 hours

The induction course to Educational Kinesiology designed for educators and the lay person having no prior experiences with techniques of applied kinesiology. Emphasis is on correcting reading
related dysfunctions through Dennison Laterality Repatterning and
crossing the midline for eyes, ears, and hand-eye coordination.

   I. THE LATERAL HEMISPHERES
      A.  The "Try" Brain (Expressive/Analytic/Language)
         1. Personality
         2. Skills
      B.  The "Reflex" Brain (receptive/gestalt/visual)
         1. Personality
         2. Skills
      C.  The Midline - Bridge or Barrier to learning
         1. Bilateral or simultaneous processing
         2. Homolateral or parallel processing

  II. BRAIN TESTING WITH AN INDICATOR MUSCLE
      A.  Preparing Yourself as a Testor
      B.  Preparing Student for Testing
      C.  "Switched On" Muscle
      D.  "Switched Off" Muscle
      E.  Anchoring With a "Switched On" Muscle

III. TESTING THE BRAIN THROUGH THE VISUAL SYSTEM
      A.  Testing Visual Organization - 4 Visual Fields
         1.  Before and After Tracking
         2.  Before and After Reading
      B.  Repatterning of Visual Organization
         1.  Figure 8's
         2.  Tracking as Anchoring
         3.  "Switched On" Reading as Positive Reinforcement

IV. TESTING BRAIN THROUGH AUDITORY SYSTEM
    A. Testing Auditory Organization - 2 Auditory Fields
        1. Language/Analytic Ear
        2. Gestalt/Tonal Ear
        3. Digit Spans (or "Spelling Bee")
    B. Repatterning Auditory Organization
        1. Repattern with the "Elephant."
        2. Anchoring Ears in 2 Positions
        3. Digit Spans (Or Other) As Anchoring


V. TESTING FOR SIMULTANEOUS BRAIN PROCESSING THROUGH WHOLE BODY MOVEMENT
    A. Testing for Simultaneous Processing
        1. Cross Crawl Across Midline
        2. Testing for "X"
    B. Testing For Preference for Parallel Processing
        1. Homolateral Crawl Avoiding Midline
        2. Testing the "II"
    C. Repatterning of Brain for More Spontaneous Movement
        1. Anchoring as "Switched On" With Cross Crawl
        2. Anchoring As "Switched On" For "X"
    D. Repatterning of Brain for Conscious Control
        1. Anchoring as "Switched Off" for Homolateral Movement
        2. Anchoring as "Switched Off" for "II"


VI. BRAIN GYM
    A. Exercises to Grow By
        1. Midline Movements
        2. Energy Flows
        3. Deepening Attitudes
    B. Evaluation
        1. Anchor positive experiences
        2. Design new programs regularly

E-K II:  PERSONALIZED WHOLE BRAIN INTEGRATION WORKSHOP
Text:  <u>Personalized Whole Brain Integration</u> by Paul Dennison,
    Ph.D, and Gail Hargrove (Revised 1985)  suggest  12 hours

A more in-depth experience of hemispheric integration techniques,
including correction of homolateral muscle systems and interpreta-
tion of brain dominance patterns.


PART 1. REVIEW OF BASIC I (E-K FOR KIDS) WITH ADDITIONAL THEORY

    I. THE LATERAL HEMISPHERES
        A.   The "Try" Brain (Expressive/Analytic/Language)
        B.   The "Reflex" Brain (receptive/gestalt/visual)
        C.   The Midline - Bridge or Barrier
        D.   Transposed Hemispheres

    II. BRAIN TESTING WITH AN INDICATOR MUSCLE
        A.   Preparing Yourself as a Testor
        B.   Preparing Student for Testing
        C.   "Switched On" Muscle
        D.   "Switched Off" Muscle
        E.   Anchoring With a "Switched On" Muscle

    III. TESTING THE BRAIN THROUGH THE VISUAL SYSTEM
        A.   Testing Visual Organization - 4 Visual Fields
            1.   Before and After Tracking
            2.   Before and After Reading
         B.   Repatterning of Visual Organization
            1.   Figure 8's
            2.   Tracking as Anchoring
            3.   "Switched On" Reading as Positive Reinforcement

    IV. TESTING BRAIN THROUGH AUDITORY SYSTEM
        A.   Testing Auditory Organization - 2 Auditory Fields
            1.   Language/Analytic Ear
            2.   Gestalt/Tonal Ear
            3.   Digit Spans (or "Spelling Bee")
        B.   Repatterning Auditory Organization
            1.   Anchoring Ears in 2 Positions
            2.   Digit Spans (Or Other) As Anchoring

V. TESTING FOR SIMULTANEOUS BRAIN PROCESSING THROUGH WHOLE BODY MOVEMENT
   A. Testing for Simultaneous Processing
      1. Cross Crawl Across Midline
      2. Testing for "X"
   B. Testing For Preference for Parallel Processing
      1. Homolateral Crawl Avoiding Midline
      2. Testing the "II"
   C. Repatterning of Brain for More Spontaneous Movement
      1. Anchoring as "Switched On" With Cross Crawl
      2. Anchoring As "Switched On" For "X"
   D. Repatterning of Brain for Conscious Control
      1. Anchoring as "Switched Off" for Homolateral Movement
      2. Anchoring as "Switched Off" for "II"

PART 2. PERSONALIZED E-K

   VI. BRAIN DOMINANCE PATTERNS
       A. Uniform
       B. Cross or Mixed
       C. Blocked
       D. Integrated

   VII. HOMOLATERAL MUSCLE CORRECTION

   VIII. BRAIN GYM
         A. Designing a Personalized Program
            1. The 3-Dimensional Brain/Body System
               a. Testing Supraspinatus (Fig Leaf) - Laterality
               b. Testing Lats (Penguin) - Back Brain/Front Brain
               c. Testing PMC (Swimmer) - Top/Bottom Brain (Centering)
            2. Exercises to Grow By
               a. Midline Movements
               b. Energy Flows
               c. Lengthening Exercises
               d. Deepening Self- Awareness
         B. Evaluation
            1. Anchor positive experiences
            2. Design new programs regularly

   IX. TEACHING PERSONAL ECOLOGY
       A. Life-Positive and Life-Negative Environments
       B. Live-Whole and Devitalized Foods
       C. "Switched On" and "Switched Off" Language

## THE INTEGRATED PERSON AND THE BRAIN HEMISPHERES
### "The whole is more than the sum of its parts"

## NEUROLOGY AND CONSCIOUSNESS

The laterally integrated person is someone who has learned how to use his two hemispheres together, as a whole system; the homolatal or "switched off" person is someone who has yet to use more than one small part of his consciousness at one given time. Our experiences determine how integrated we become. Unfortunately, because of the homolateral behaviors and attitudes in our society, most of us do not realize the level of integration available to us. Instead of the spontaneous, joyous, life we could have as human beings, we function as limited machines in controlled and rigid patterns. The disabilities and dys-eases that people experience are symptoms of failure to achieve the integrated state. After one learns to use the whole brain, disabilities start to disappear.

## THE BRAIN

In order for the right and left brain to work in integrated fashion, the two brain hemispheres are interconnected by the corpus callosum, an intricate bundle of nerve fibers. In infancy, a complex system of switches is developed during the first few months of life. Ideally, as we first creep, and then crawl, we begin to synchronize and integrate information so that the two hemispheres can work together through life in harmony and coordination. One hemisphere can take over for the other and can also operate on its own side to process a given task. To learn a new task easily, both sides of the brain need to be involved in the operation.

The right brain hemisphere controls the left side of the body and the consciousness of the left eye and ear. Likewise, the left brain hemisphere controls the right side of the body and the right eye and ear. The nerves to the muscles and sense organs cross over from the controlling brain hemisphere. When one side of the brain is in control, the other side either cooperates and coordinates its movements with the controlling hemisphere, or it may "switch off" and block integration.

8

# PERCEPTION AND REALITY

We may perceive our world from two entirely different perspectives
or points of view; either as a whole (through the gestalt hemisphere) or one piece at a time (through the analytic hemisphere)
Our awareness of what we know depends upon the hemispheres of the
brain. Although neurologically more complicated, the metaphor of
the receptive/gestalt view of reality and the expressive/analytic
view of reality as two distinct systems can help us to understand
and make changes in function!

## RECEPTIVE/GESTALT CONSCIOUSNESS

The receptive brain, usually in the right hemisphere, is wholistic
and grasps the biggest picture or "whole" available, rather than
perceiving the parts and putting them back together.  It is the
receptive gestalt brain which specializes in the recognition of
faces, an ability most people still have long after they have
forgotten someone's name.  The receptive gestalt brain is respon-
sible for other long term visual memories, orientation in space,
rhythm and tone, body awareness, and artistic abilities (such as
sense of color and spatial relationships).  This brain is necessary when we need to process information in recognizable "chunks"
where no analysis or linear, sequential operation is necessary.
This receptive brain receives information passively, without
judgment or sense of limitation.  This brain contains our connection with our bodies, nature, and our surroundings; that is,
this is the "context" from which the Self derives meaning.

## EXPRESSIVE/ANALYTIC CONSCIOUSNESS

The expressive/analytic brain, usually located in the left hemisphere, has an entirely different perception of reality.  It is
critical, judgmental, and acutely aware of time and survival. It
works in terms of goals, language, and self-expression.  It processes in computerlike fashion breaking down information into tiny
bits which it can sequence and order, one at a time. This analytic
brain is the language center where the ability to speak and understand verbal information is generated and stored. This hemisphere
contains the Common Integrative Area (near Broca's point) where
the learning process is completed and comprehension takes place.
The Common Integrative Area is activated when experiences are
internalized and become a part of the Ego.

## THE ONE-SIDED STATE

The first step towards the integrated state is bilateral integration, where one has access to both right and left hemispheres at
the same time, and, therefore, both eyes, both ears, and both
sides of the body. The homolateral person is limited to "one-sided" thinking because he has access to only one side of the brain
at one time, and must "switch off" one side each time he wants to
use the other, in alternating fashion. Although he can be adept at
this "parallel processing", the homolateral person always experiences a coordination problem, at some level, depending upon the
severity of his disability. Whether it affects his eyes, ears, or
body as a whole, he doesn't seem to use the two sides of the brain
together through the corpus callosum as nature intended.

For example, this might be the child who switches off the analy-
tic/language ear in school. He becomes so absorbed in the gestalt,
the intonation of the teacher's voice or outside noises, that he
loses all sense of the meaning of the words.  As a reader, he
might switch off his gestalt eye, therefore breaking down the
words into sounds but unable to blend them into whole units, or to
register them in his long-term, visual memory.

The homolateral person is confused (and therefore tests weak with
muscle testing) by bilateral activity.  Walking, swimming, run-
ning, or jogging, all require increased conscious effort and conscious control, which cause him to switch off the gestalt brain.
Instead of relaxing and energizing him, these activities seem to
bring him further frustration and may even lead to injury.  His
tendency may be to avoid large muscle activity or to place high
demands on his body to achieve through competition or goal setting, as opposed to the pure intrinisic reward of joyful movement.

The homolateral person moves in space so that the spine, cranial
bones, and sacrum do not move together.  This results in the
blockage of cerebrospinal fluid  which should nourish and cool
the whole brain from back to front.  The homolateral person moves
in more rigid, blocked, or controlled patterns, often without
breathing, which inhibits the integration process.  The homolateral person functions mostly from the back brain.  This is where
incoming sensations are processed, where motor activity generated
by these sensations is initiated, and where analysis and storage
of experience takes place.  The homolateral person can learn and

repeat material, often quite skillfully.  In fact, this person thrives on the familiarity of automatic or conditioned behavior.  However, the homolateral person is denied that true learning experience  when something becomes uniquely one's own.

THE WHOLE BRAIN STATE

Too much attention and adulation has been accorded the gestalt or "right" brain in interpreting recent brain research.  The gestalt brain's contribution to information processing and the proper functioning of the autonomic nervous system is undeniable.  However, it is not an either/or situation as some learning systems might suggest.  The gestalt brain's functions must certainly be recognized and developed for the realization of optimal potential; however, the gestalt brain has been given credit for what is actually the work of the Integrated Brain.  We must remember that the gestalt brain alone is totally passive, receptive only, and without the ability to make discriminative responses and to express itself; just as the analytic brain alone can do little more than compare, criticize, and regurgitate information.

What most people have attributed to the "right" brain is really the result of back brain/front brain integration which takes place in the Common Integrative Area, a part of the "left" brain, not the "right" at all.  The integrated person expresses herself or himself from a context, through this language area.  He knows who he is, believes what he is saying or doing, and expresses himself fluently.  No performance, be it reading comprehension, painting, dancing, or other can belong to the performer until this level of integration is achieved.

The laterally integrated person is able to process information simultaneously, with both hemispheres "switched on" at the same time.  He or she can move and think at the same time; read with the writer's hand; speak with the listener's ear, and commit to any task and bring her whole person to it.  In fact, the integrated person thrives on the new, the spontaneous, and the creative.  Even the most simple undertaking becomes a joyful opportunity for full self-expression.

# A PRACTICAL LOOK AT DOMINANCE
## "In the beginning, there was the opposable thumb...."


## DOMINANCE PATTERNS AND PERSONALITY

Since the book <u>Switching On</u> was written, we have learned much more
about the concept of "dominance", how to explain it, how to test
it, and how to talk to people about it. We are actually pioneers
in the field of brain dominance. Although its existence has been
recognized for years, nothing positive or constructive has ever
been done with the concept, and it has been ignored by most authorities in education, psychology and medicine.

Now, with E-K dominance testing we are able to identify the unique
dominance pattern of the individual. In E-K, our intention is to
discover the inherited "personality" dominance of the individual
as manifested through his preferred eye, ear, hand and brain hemisphere. We recognize that there are many learning styles, represented by these dominance patterns, which have, heretofore, been
ignored by educators. Not only can we now help these children to
reach their full and special potential; but, since these patterns
are often familial, we can also counsel parents about the gifts
and needs that they share.

## ARE WE ALL "LANGUAGE BRAINED" DOMINANT?

One important difference between Educational Kinesiology and other
systems is the meaning of the term "dominant hemisphere". In much
of the literature, the dominant hemisphere is synonymous with the
"left" brain or the side of the brain in control of language and
expression. Experts talk about a dominant hemisphere, as if the
language brain is more important, and they talk about a non-dominant hemisphere, implying that the "right" brain or gestalt is not
as important as the "left".

Using handedness as a determining factor, these experts believe
that most people are "left" brained and speech-center dominant,
since right-handedness exists in 80% of the population. This sta-
tistic also just reinforces their thinking that the language brain
is, indeed, the dominant brain. Granted it is loss of speech that
is often more upsetting to one's normal life than loss of movement
in case of stroke or accident. However, there really is no "better" dominance for healthy people, nor has nature selected one
side of the brain to dominate.

On the contrary, our research, using our muscle tests, proves that there are "language brain personalities" and "gestalt brain personalities" in equal numbers in the population. Fifty percent of all human beings are "left-brained" and the other fifty percent are "right-brained". Handedness is not a reliable determinant of dominance at all! Scientists have recognized, that in the animal kingdom, half the creatures are right-pawed, and half of them are left-pawed! These same scientists are having problems reconciling this finding with the ratio of right and left "paws" in the human population.

## HANDEDNESS AND THE CONSCIOUS MIND

For us it is perfectly obvious and explainable. How do human beings differ from animals? Humans are uniquely blessed with a conscious mind that learns to do new things and to use new tools with intention, control, and fine motor skills. This control and near point focus originates in the  hemisphere where speech and language also originate. For most of us, this is the left hemisphere. As we activate our left brains, especially if we are one-sided or homolateral (defined elsewhere in E-K literature), we will use the right hand, even if it isn't the hand controlled by our dominant brain! It is survival in the human environment and the need for self-consciousness and control  which creates the right-handedness. Brain dominance is hereditary and determines one's personality and temperament. Handedness can be learned, but brain dominance is permanent.

## THE DOMINANT EYE

One's dominant eye is apparently a more reliable determinant of brain dominance than the dominant hand. Most "right-brained" people are left-eye dominant. They are also usually left-ear dominant as well. As discussed in Switching On, people who are right-handed and left-eyed and/or left-eared are "mixed dominant" and comprise the dyslexic population, both the literal (reading and writing) and figurative (movement, emotional stress) midline. (See Switching On for more details on this aspect.)

## TRANSPOSED HEMISPHERES

Another difference between Educational Kinesiology and other systems that talk about brain dominance has to do with location of the language brain.  Neurologists have recognized that a small percentage of the population, mostly left handers, have the language, speech centers, in the right hemisphere instead of the left.  E-K calls this state "Transposed Hemispheres".  E-K research suggests that far more than the 5% figure represented in neurological literature have language on the right, including many right-handers!

In E-K dominance testing, we take into account not only whether a person is right hemispheric dominant or left hemispheric dominant, but also whether she is language or gestalt dominant.  In other words, our student may be left-gestalt dominant instead of left language dominant.  Likewise, she may be right-language dominant instead of right-gestalt dominant!

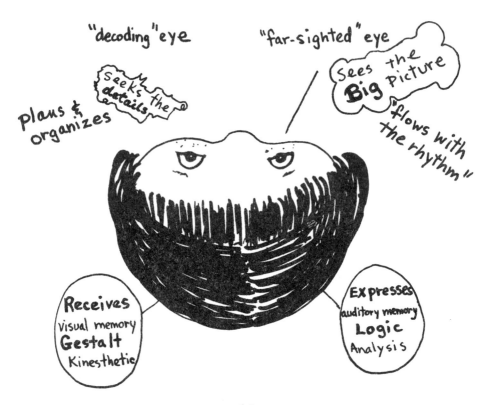

"The switched off kid learns that life doesn't count at school.
The switched on kid can count on school and life to be one"

## CROSS OR MIXED DOMINANCE

Over fifty percent of the learning disabled population is cross or
mixed dominant. This dominance pattern invites confusion and dis-
organization, especially in the homolateral state and especially
for fine motor skills. The person with this pattern is dominant
with the hand on one side of the body and the eye and/or ear on
the other. The hemisphere which is "on" for the hand is not the
hemisphere for the eye. This is especially difficult when a child
is "left" eye dominant and right-handed. His compensation to read
"left to right" is to switch off the dominant eye in order to lead
with the right eye. Visual memory and gestalt skills are, therefore, not available to the learner.

## JIM - MIXED DOMINANCE

Jim is a management executive, age 33, who wants to improve his
slow reading skills. He explains that he has never really enjoyed
reading as it is such a struggle for him. His dominance pattern
is right-gestalt brain dominant, right-handed, left-eyed, and
right-eared.

## JIM'S READING

As Jim reads across the page his eyes jump uncontrollably instead
of flowing back and forth from line to line. He stops every few
lines to think or to reread something he has already forgotten.
His reading voice is a strained, high-pitched, wail rather than
his natural speaking voice. He sometimes stumbles over the punc-
tuation, or gasps for air in the middle of a phrase. When asked
to explain what he has read, he is unable to paraphrase, searching
his analytic short-term memory instead for the exact words of the
author. He confides that he has wonderful ideas, but seems to for-
get them the moment he picks up a pencil to write with his right
hand.

15

Jim is the "typical" dyslexic reader, switching off his gestalt dominant personality and far-sighted left eye to read. He is homolateral and has survived the educational system by "parallel" processing, alternating from hemisphere to hemisphere, memorizing and "cramming" his way through printed verbal material.

After repatterning, Jim's prior effort to use his non-dominant language brain made his integration that much faster. Already skilled in the mechanics of reading, he is now able to bring imagination and drama to his oral presentations as never before. (An aside — he says the ideas are getting onto his paper now.)

JIM — MIXED DOMINANCE
READING PATTERN, BEFORE E-K

16

# BLOCKED DOMINANCE

The "blocked dominant" pattern is a totally new discovery which evolved out of E-K research. In E-K we define a person's dominance in terms of genetically predetermined personality traits as confirmed by muscle testing. We have discovered that many people are dominant in one hemisphere, but use not only the hand controlled by the non-dominant hemisphere, as the mixed dominant person, but the eye and ear as well. As a result, for reading, writing, listening, and most academic functions, they are subject to "switching off" their dominant brain and personality whenever they are under stress and "trying" to do well.

## LISA- GESTALT BLOCKED DOMINANT

An example is Lisa, an incredibly talented artist and musician. Her paintings are enchanting, and when she plays her flute, one feels the life energy swelling in one's chest. Lisa was tested and found to be a "blocked" dominant personality. She is "right-gestalt brained", and also right-handed, right-eyed, and right-eared. How does this information help her?

The year that Lisa was tested, she was "homolateral", and not using her dominant gestalt hemisphere at all. She had stopped practicing her music. She was a senior in high school and was competing academically with hundreds for admission to a prestigious ivy league school. The more Lisa studied, the more stressed, compulsive, mean, and difficult she became, to both herself and those around her.

Miraculously, she survived two major automobile accidents where she had been the driver. Lisa could not access her dominant right gestalt brain even to drive while in this homolateral state of mind. E-K corrections to help her become heterolateral and the advice that she return to her art and music helped her to achieve more hemispheric integration in her life. Now in college, she is able to access both her highly trained but non-dominant language brain and her naturally endowed gestalt right brain. She is living proof that the whole is more than the sum of its parts.

LISA – GESTALT BLOCKED
(BEFORE E–K)

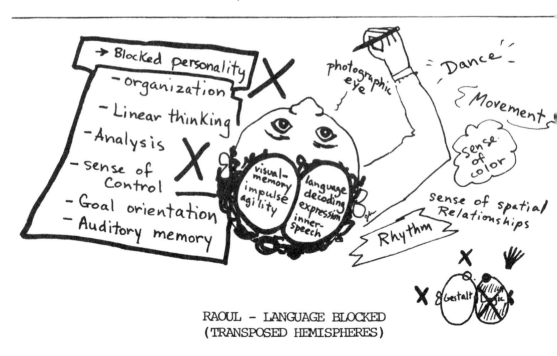

RAOUL – LANGUAGE BLOCKED
(TRANSPOSED HEMISPHERES)

## RAOUL- LANGUAGE BLOCKED DOMINANT

Raoul, a dyslexic in junior high school, was "blocked dominant" and a most interesting case, indeed. Raoul is right-handed and right-eyed, so "mixed dominance" was ruled out by school authorities as a factor in his learning problems. E-K testing revealed that he has transposed hemispheres, that is, his language-speech centers are in the right hemisphere, not the left. He is right-language brain dominant, which, for him, means a preference for linguistic and linear thinking, but he has been relying, instead, on his non-dominant, visual-gestalt brain whenever he writes or attempts to read; tasks which require the activation of his right hand and right eye.

Unlike most dyslexics, who switch off the visual memory centers, Raoul has been switching off his language and inner-speech centers. He has an extensive vocabulary and scored above average on intelligence test measures, but could not remember or enjoy what he read, no matter how he tried. Since he was homolateral in his development as well, he did not yet know how to use both hemispheres together, at a given time.

E-K corrections, and the advice to practice consciously using the left side of the body (through bi-hemispheric drawing and dancing) to activate his right brain helped Raoul to become a better listener, and his memory dramatically improved. Already skilled at the mechanical, receptive, aspects of reading, Raoul was soon able to apply these skills to more complex materials. He appreciates how important it is to have both hemispheres working for him when he is at school, and does his exercises faithfully.

## "UNIFORM" DOMINANCE

Mark is a first grade child who reads at the fourth grade level. He is in the top group in all academic subjects, without making any apparent effort. He is the "teacher's pet" because he is always ready, follows directions and understands everything she says in class.

Mark is left, analytic brain dominant, and all right side dominant (for eye, ear, and hand). When Mark's left brain is on, he is activating the right side of his body. Since this situation activates his dominant language brain and dominant eye, ear, and hand, he can decode, write, and listen to language without much neurological conflict. By mental age 6 1/2, his gestalt brain had developmentally taken over the automatic movement of his right hand and right eye, so he is able to cross the midline adequately, without "switching off" his gestalt right brain. He is able to see the whole and the parts together; to anticipate, remember, and visualize. His dominance pattern has few, if any, learning complications. He is "an easy going kid" his mother tells us and "very adaptable".

"Uniform" Dominance does not guarantee an effortless academic experience, however. For children like Mark, the biggest challenge may be language activation to the exclusion of the gestalt. If he is denied positive, enjoyable movement experiences, he may not learn to interact, to use his imagination and creativity, or to be able to relax and let go. He may have stress from his language brain, related to time, goals, or self-criticism. He may need to be perfect. He may try too hard. When Mark is unable to access his gestalt hemisphere for fluid, easy body movement, he may become stiff and robot-like, with mechnical body movement.

## UNIFORM DOMINANT-WRITING DEVELOPMENT

Sometimes children like Mark, who have "uniform" dominance, are so well rewarded for switching off the gestalt brain in school that, by the time they are in third grade, they lose the advantage they had in the earlier grades. They often know the answers but cannot write them down because they try too hard; that is, they allow the language, analytic brain to control the writing hand so that movement becomes awkward as they vascillate between thought and action. In this one-sided state they cannot express what they know because their language brain, which can only do one thing at one time, is involved in the mechanics of writing instead of thinking and expressing. They cannot access their long-term memories to retrieve the information that they thought they knew.

## UNIFORM DOMINANT-READING DEVELOPMENT

If children like Mark try too hard, they may read with the right eye only and become easily fatigued. They cannot always "gestalt" the words from the context of the material, overly relying on their superior decoding abilities. They may read with a high, shrill voice which shows the stress of the language brain analyzing the text. These children can think much faster than they can read, mechanically, and are easily bored by this type of information processing. Uniform dominant children do not usually have the symptoms of dyslexia, such as reversals and transpositions of letters, experienced by cross dominant children, because their right eye is their dominant personality eye and moves from left to right naturally. The joy of reading depends, however, on the integrated state where the gestalt eye and brain work together with the language eye and brain.

## UNIFORM DOMINANT-SPELLING DEVELOPMENT

Children with uniform dominance tend to make spelling errors which show that they sound out words rather than visualizing them. They cannot always recognize that a word "looks wrong". They don't always seem to sense the similarities between the roots of new words and those they already know. They may repeat the same spelling errors, unable to associate the word they are writing with the same word in long term memory. They may not be able to make use of rhythm clues such as rhymes and syllabication.

## UNIFORM DOMINANCE AND ACADEMIC ACHIEVEMENT

Uniform dominant people tend to compensate well in school and can achieve academically with relatively little stress. They are usually good workers, although they may lack imagination. They sometimes have difficulty expressing their feelings and may be unable to associate creativity and feeling with work or success. They may not see the connection between life and school, and, later, life and work.

DOMINANCE PATTERNS/ SOME IMPLICATIONS FOR THE HOMOLATERAL PERSON

It may be interesting to consider that the common integration area of the brain is in the language center where expressive functions are internalized and made a part of the Self. This area is where one experiences "who I am" and "what I want to do with myself." This area may be blocked by anyone who is homolateral. In this state it may be difficult or stressful to access language abilities for someone who is:
1. Functioning from the gestalt dominant brain (like Jim).
2. Blocked language dominant (like Raoul).
3. In an overenergy state (see E-K For Kids or Advanced Manual).


By the same token, the ability to relax, experience a context for one's life, to be attuned to one's intuition, and to "see the big picture" may be "blocked" for the person who is homolateral and is:
1. Blocked gestalt dominant (like Lisa).
2. Functioning from his language dominant brain (like Mark).
3. In an overenergy state, or in a state of extreme stress (see Advanced Manual).

22

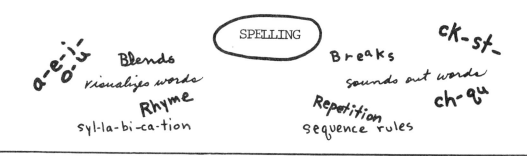

**SPELLING**

a-e-i-o-u    Blends        Breaks    cK-st-

visualizes words      sounds out words

Rhyme        Repetition    ch-qu

syl-la-bi-ca-tion      sequence rules

---

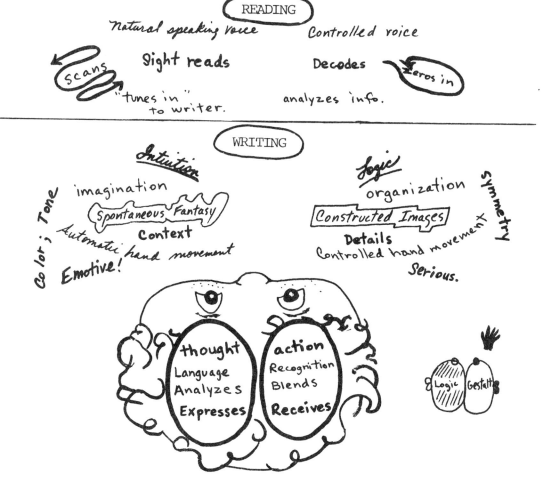

**READING**

Natural speaking voice      Controlled voice

Sight reads      Decodes    Zeros in

Scans

"tunes in" to writer.      analyzes info.

---

**WRITING**

Intuition        Logic

imagination      organization    symmetry

Spontaneous Fantasy      Constructed Images

Color; Tone    Context      Details

Automatic hand movement      Controlled hand movement

Emotive!      Serious.

thought    action
Language    Recognition
Analyzes    Blends
Expresses    Receives

Logic   Gestalt

MARK — UNIFORM DOMINANCE

23

PERSONALITY DOMINANCE AND LEARNING STRATEGY
"using only 5% of our brain's potential?!!"


WHAT DO YOU MEAN YOU CAN'T READ?

As in most modern cultures, the ability to read is a decisive factor in how well we will function in our everyday lives.  We are de-
pendent on our reading skills for everything from driving an automobile, to reading food labels, to holding any well-paying job.
For those who have difficulties with the basic reading skills,
this factor alone can hinder their ultimate progress in life.

However, there is much more to reading than even these basic
skills.  In E-K, we define the ideal reader from a more broad
perspective.

Steve is a good E-K reader.  He muscle tests strong on all the basic skills of eye movement across the midline and decoding and en-
coding language (the ability to hear his own voice, or those of
the imagined characters).  For Steve, these skills happen automatically.  That is, the gestalt reflex for them to happen takes
place without any conscious effort on his part.

Steve's integrated brain is free to imagine, create, and play in-
ternal games of feedback about the characters, the author's meaning, his own similar experiences, and so on.  Steve is a good
driver, as he takes this skill at feedback and feedforward of information into his ability to react quickly in any situation.
This carries over into his job as manager of an insurance company,
where he is admired and well paid for his ability to "think on his
feet," and to be skilled at anticipating problems or opportunities
before they are apparent to others.

Like Mark, in the section on Dominance, Steve has a uniform dominance pattern (left language brain, all right-sided).  He seems
to have "inherited" these abilities.  He says he has always had a
"healthy" disposition and was an easy learner - never experiencing
eye stress or mental stress in school, as some children do.  What
does his dominance pattern have to do with this ease of learning
that has contributed to his good feelings of self-esteem and trust
in his abilities?

## READING AND MOVEMENT

Perhaps to find the answer, we should consider what happens to
most people we test when they read, and our E-K view about Western
languages.

The English language, as other Western languages, is based upon
analytic, phonetic, "language brain" activating symbols, (as opposed to pictographs or more "gestalt brain" symbols, as in Chin-
ese). These English symbols move from left to right across the
page, opposite to the flow of movement for the gestalt brain, and
are most easily decoded when the right eye is the "language brain"
or "analytic" eye, and does the leading and decoding (as in the
case of Steve).

## THE HAND THAT HANDLES

The only way for this to happen is for there to be a certain level
of integration between the writing hand, the listening ear, and
the looking eye. For a reader with uniform dominance, such as
Steve, who has accomplished basic neurological pre-reading skills,
there is usually little conflict in the integrity of eye, ear and
hand.

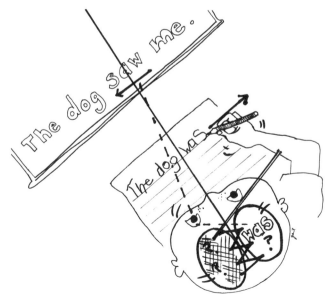

SWITCHING OFF ON THE MIDLINE

In order to read, to write, to spell, to listen, or to be integrated for any activity, for that matter, one must be able to cross
the midline" which connects right and left brain, the two opposing
polarities of the body. The left brain and right hand have a positive polarity and the right brain and left hand have a negative
polarity. The midline is either a bridge or a barrier to learning, depending upon polarity imbalances within one's system. When
right and left brains communicate spontaneously, working together
at one time, then the midline becomes a bridge, connecting positive and negative energy fields. When right and left brains must
take turns working, the connection is broken, and the midline becomes a barrier.

By mental age 6½, the right eye and hand should be able to move a-
cross the midline from left to right without switching off the vis-
ual/gestalt brain, thereby allowing the student to do both language brain and gestalt brain activating tasks! (See Switching On
for more information on this). However, for the homolateral student with mixed or blocked dominance, or the student with transposed hemispheres, this does not happen as easily or as completely
as it should, and some learning problems are the inevitable result.

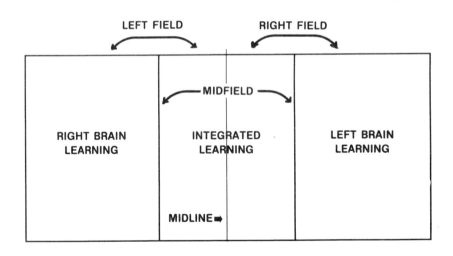

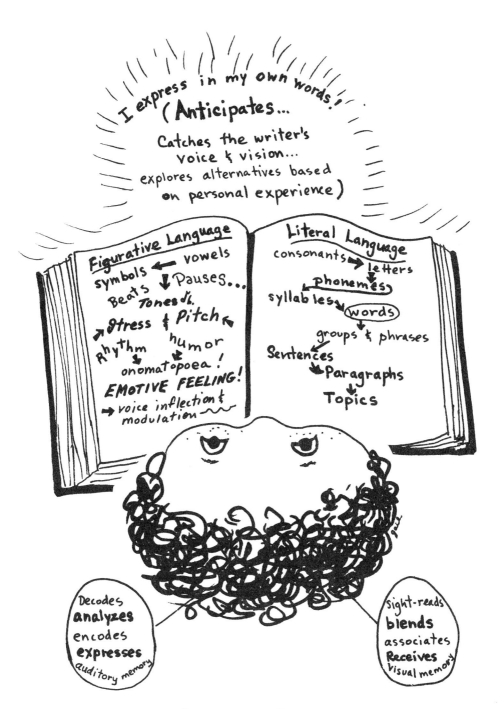

THE "SWITCHED ON" READER

27

# DOMINANT EYE AND EAR PROFILES
## "Experience is in the 'eye of the beholder'; the ear of the listener"

## THE MIND'S EYE

### TYRONE- GESTALT EYE DOMINANT

What does it mean to be visual/gestalt eye dominant?    This is the child, like Tyrone (age 5), whose visual experience is shaped by his gestalt brain.    Tyrone is the "far-sighted" child, who pays more attention to distance, movement, and the "whole picture" than he does to near-point activity.  He is intrigued by color, tone, shape, feeling, more than he is by details.  He is usually wearing solid colors, and often bright or unusual colors.

Tyrone's play tends to emphasize more large, whole body movement, than small motor coordination. He goes for the slide or the swing. He likes to run and move, and isn't as happy sitting still and focusing in close on one thing.  He likes to build with large blocks or sand and is very kinesthetically oriented.  He is warm and friendly, always ready to touch or hug, or to hit if the situation arises.  He is happier outside and always seems to be looking out over the group, even in the classroom.

Tyrone is adept at putting together mechanical things.  He has a "sense" of how they go, without being able to explain  his ability to make them work.  Tyrone, like many other gestalt eye dominant children, prefers to work in an environment that is visually and emotionally in "order".

### MIA - ANALYTIC EYE DOMINANT

Mia's visual experience is shaped by her dominant analytic eye, her choice for focusing, and her language/analytic brain.  Mia, also age 5, pays more attention to small details, like the organization of the doll house furniture, or the placement of dolls and stuffed animals for her game.  She likes finite details and is neat and orderly in the small area in which she plays, but seems unaware or unconcerned with organization of her larger environment.

Mia's vision tends to be "near-sighted"; that is, she can find the one puzzle piece she needs out of the box, or the perfect button or bead out of the button box. She likes to draw and use tools. She enjoys cutting and pasting. She likes to copy and is good at analyzing form. She is fascinated by taking apart mechanical things, to study and analyze, but is usually unable to put them back together as a whole; nor does she have the interest.

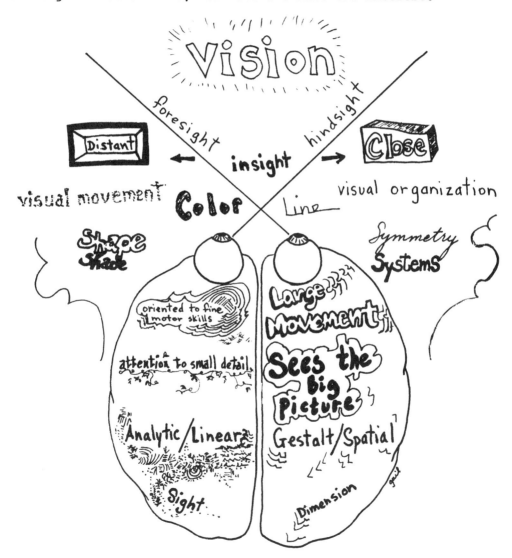

# SOUND AND SENSE

## TYRONE'S DOMINANT GESTALT EAR

Tyrone's dominant ear is his gestalt/tonal ear. This is reflected by his language development. His sentences are short and to the point. He often expresses himself in non-verbal ways - relying on gesture, facial expression, and body posture to make his feelings known. He is quite good at "listening" to such clues as well, from others. He sometimes seems to expect others to know what he wants without explaining himself! He also has an ability to imitate voice, body posture, expressions and gesture - sometimes to the point of exasperation. He has a clever sense of humor.

Tyrone is very adept at making guttural sounds, train imitations, and the whistles of birds that no one else can do. In class, he often seems not to be listening, as he is easily distracted by non-language sounds, like the street traffic, dogs barking, loud noises or talking from the other classroom. He loves music and has a good sense of rhythm and movement. He seems to enjoy listening to poetry more than any other language skill activity.

## MIA'S LANGUAGE/ANALYTIC DOMINANT EAR

Mia is dominant for her language/analytic ear. When she and Susan play, Mia enjoys going into great verbal detail about how the play will go, and what will happen in which sequence. Mia likes to use language to analyze things, and can discuss a dream or event in great detail. She looks for verbal clues to know what is going to happen next. She likes to read, silently or aloud, and listens avidly at storytime. She talks and sings to herself. She already likes to express herself through made-up stories. She also likes poetry, loving the words, and can memorize quickly.

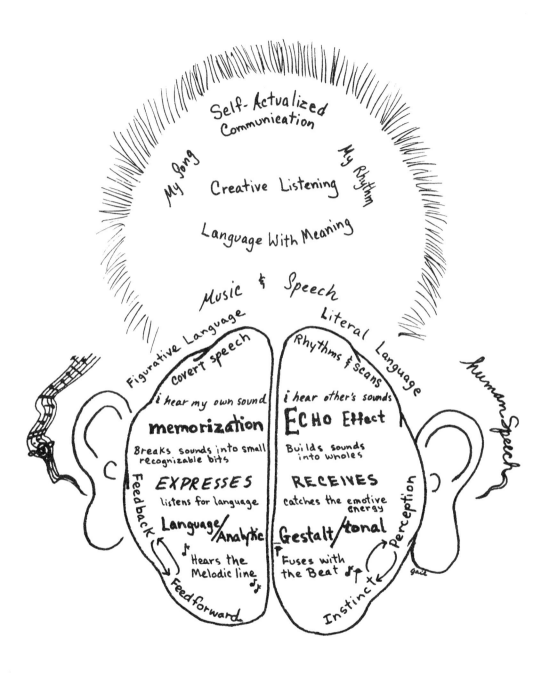

SOUND AND THE HEMISPHERES

SUMMARY

Mia and Tyrone are good examples of these dominant patterns as they are still functioning at the homolateral stage, and have not yet developed enough compensations, or "switched off" behaviors to block the inherited characteristics of their dominance patterns. In both cases, these children are influenced by having similar dominance for eye, ear, and brain hemisphere. However, looking at their overall patterns of behavior and preferred choices about learning helps us to understand how dominance patterns affect our personalities and learning abilities, as well as the difficulties faced by dominance patterns, like Tyrone's, that don't fit the demands of the academic situation.

SPECIAL THINGS ABOUT THE CHILD WITH TRANSPOSED HEMISPHERES

Seth has transposed hemispheres. His left eye is his analytic eye. When he reads, he leads with his right, gestalt eye. At age 7, he is a sight reader, using his right gestalt/visual eye and long-term memory for reading. For the next two or so years, this decoding stage of reading will be the most difficult for Seth. If he switches off the left eye and language brain, he may not ever learn to decode words. He may have to read things twice over in order to get the language, and will likely have difficulty with spelling clues.

However, if he continues to develop his reading skills, and gets past the decoding stage, he may become a speed reader. Perhaps he will be able to see whole blocks of thoughts at a given time, and clue into the writer's "wave length" with that gestalt eye and brain. He may, like some people we have tested with transposed hemispheres, develop a "photographic memory" for his reading, able to remember the exact page or section where something is written.

Equally important to understanding Seth is the realization that his hemisphere for automatic movement is in the left brain which governs the movement of his right, writing hand!

He uses his artistic, visual eye for reading, as well as for writing. Reading and writing may not develop simultaneously as they should because the ability to read by sight and imagination will not help with analyzing words and letters into smaller bits. Once Seth masters the mechanics of writing his true creativity will appear in his written work.

32

# EDUCATION AND POSITIVE MUSCLE TESTING
## "Freedom only exists for the choice-maker"


## E-K AND STRESS FREE LEARNING

Would we be willing to let go of the notions that learning must be slow and tedious, that life need be a struggle, that the adult world must be prepared for with fortitude and resignation? Can we leap into a "new" and easy way of learning, like the infant "leaps" into the world joyfully absorbing the wonder and growing with it?

## EDUCATIONAL KINESIOLOGY

Our experience is that learning happens best through the spontaneous growth of the individual. Within him the seeds of freedom, choice, and global learning are already well sown. The very baseline of choice-making is to operate with both cerebral hemispheres switched on so that true options exist. Educational Kinesiology is a wonderful tool for supporting growth and reawakening innate potentials. Through it, we can guide the individual to polish his or her unique talents.


## E-K AND SPONTANEOUS LEARNING

For those of us in E-K, learning is that magical thing that takes place in a split second, that changes us forever, allowing us to move, and think in a new way. In E-K we believe that no matter how many times we repeat a "learned" task, if a better way of doing it is presented, and the whole brain/body system experiences the ease and joy of the new way, all former patterns can be released in a moment. This, for us, is learning.

Nine-year-old Aisha sits at her desk after her first E-K session. She automatically chooses to move her paper from the far right visual field, where for three years she has been twisting and struggling to write, to the midfield where she is able to write without pain or tension. This has happened by some shift within Aisha, possible now through her E-K exercises, and not through any verbal suggestion on our part. This, to us in E-K, is learning.

Thirteen-year-old Donald comes to us after hundreds of hours of cross crawl patterning and a diagnosis of "brain damage". Twenty minutes of Midline Movements and Dennison Repatterning and he is crossing the visual and body/motor coordination midline with ease! This is the first real step for Donald, and the true joy of learning with E-K.

## TEACHING THROUGH MUSCLE RESPONSE

What does education really mean? To us it means providing possibilities for growth and anchoring growth-oriented choices. We believe muscle testing is one of the best rewards possible for a person. When Susan's weak muscle test becomes strong during a session, it teaches her that she has "learned" something that enhances her physical well being. It offers that her whole brain is in harmony with this learning; that this new thing has been learned without conflict, stress, or excessive "trying", and that correct learning is a pleasurable and natural thing to do. It also teaches her that learning enhances emotional well being as well as physical comfort and energy level, and that learning can be specific to her and her unique needs.

## INTUITION AND BODY LANGUAGE

Moreover, when we help Justin to communicate with his "inner self" in this way, he intuits many things: that his negative physical and emotional behavior patterns have been established out of past "successful" patterns that are no longer wins for him; that he has the "ability to respond" in a new way that is more appropriate and will use more of his physical/emotional or energetic potential; that unconscious patterns are always his efforts to do his best at a survival level to protect and enhance his own life.

Moreover, our partnership with him in communicating with his body may already begin to open the way for him to greater mind/body communication in every day life. That is, to the extent that Justin transfers this session to everyday experience, the better he can listen to his gestalt unconscious signals and to his intuition, living from a more whole-brained perspective.

34

# MUSCLE TESTING

> "By the age of 3, we have already
> set the stage for how we will learn
> for the rest of our lives"

## CHANGE OUR BODIES; CHANGE OUR MINDS

To change a neurological or learned response, by oneself, is a very difficult, perhaps impossible task! Learned things become habits, and habits (especially those that helped us master developmental tasks) are hard to break. Even if a better way presents itself, the original habit will often persevere.

We make our early choices about movement by imitating and responding to those we love. These movements (and neurological reflexes) are reinforced, and we build a lifetime of more conscious choices upon these. Imagine! We actually come to believe these habits are an integral part of who we are, they sometimes become so self-invested!

## TESTOR AND TESTEE: A PARTNERSHIP

Every authority figure anchors growth patterns with touch, looks, or tone of voice. We are constantly nurturing and supporting the successes (and failures!) of others, by our responses to them. As teachers, it is our responsibility to polish ourselves to teach in the most positive ways we can. Muscle testing is one of the best, deepest, and least intrusive ways we know of to establish rapport and communication with another human, and to give them permission to break through their present level of homeostasis.

## INTERPRETATION OF THE MUSCLE TEST

In E-K, remember we are not really "testing muscle strength". Our intention is to test brain response. We are interested in whether or not the brain is able to send a constant signal at the same time the muscle is being tested. We are aware not only of the "switched on" and "switched off" muscle, but also the level of "switching on". That is, a strong muscle is our signal that the reflex brain is "on". This strong muscle is an automatic response on the part of the body to survive and protect itself.

The "switched off" muscle means this automatic system is under stress. Probably all the energy is going someplace other than the muscle! However, each time your student is tested and corrrected on a task (like eye movement) the brain/body circuit for that task gets strengthened. This is why her tests become stronger and more automatic each time you "anchor" her on her ability to do the task correctly. At the point of anchoring, we are anchoring for greater whole brain integration.


RITUAL IN DAILY LIFE

Ritual and ceremony are a universal part of human experience in every known culture. Ritual is used in healing and in rites of passage to imprint change; for example from childhood into man-hood, or from single status into marriage. Even going to school, with its report cards, promotions, and graduations, is a ritual with which we are all familiar.

Muscle testing in E-K is a sacred ritual. Even though we are of-ten playful with it, we never "make light" in our intention. We have the highest respect for the brain/body's ability to heal it-self and resume or continue growth when freed of blocks that have caused stagnation. We know that every muscle test is a reminder of the reality of our body's deeper intelligence and our unlimited potentials, and every muscle anchoring is a committment to a high-er level of functioning.

# HOW WE LET MOVEMENT MOVE US
## "Life is movement and movement is life"

## TRADITIONAL PATTERNING-DOMAN AND DELACATO

Cross-crawling, or patterning, has been recognized for many years
as a technique to restore neurological functioning when there has
been brain damage. It has proven effective in vision training as
practiced by developmental optometrists as well. It was during
the 1960's, that Drs. Doman and Delacato announced that, in addition to reversing brain damage, children who experienced their
patterning program could learn to read better as well. Crawling
instantly became popular at many schools across the nation. Unfortunately, educators could not replicate these results in inde-
pendent research studies with children in the classroom, and crawling, as well as other movement experience programs were, once a-
gain, relegated to the physical education departments.

## CRAWLING ALONE PROVES NOT ENOUGH

Crawling has obviously helped many people and it has disappointed
many people as well. Crawling should be the most perfect brain
balancing exercise, and, theoretically, it is. Since it requires
both cerebral hemispheres to be activated to complete the crawling step, each brain operating the opposite side of the body; the
more one crawls, the better integrated and balanced he should become. However, the human nervous system is not quite so simplis-
tic.

Because of its unique ability to study the relationship of movement and brain function with muscle testing, Educational Kinesiology is now able to explain why cross-crawling has helped some
people and not others and why crawling in the classroom has proven
unreliable as an educational tool. Further, E-K research into
cross-crawl has resulted in a correction procedure, known as
Dennison Laterality Repatterning. This procedure, if practiced as
taught in E-K Basic Workshops, makes cross-crawl the effective tool
that it ideally should be in balancing the brain for improved academic performance as well as for physical, mental, and spiritual
health.

## GESTALT DOMINANCE FOR MOVEMENT

Crawling seems only to be of therapeutic benefit to those who learn it early, in infancy, before the left-brain develops its sense of conscious awareness. When people who crept and crawled as babies cross-crawl, they test gestalt movement/reflex-brain dominant for the movement of their bodies, freeing their language analytic/try-brain to learn new things. When people have to learn to crawl later in life, they tend to be too self-conscious and aware of their bodies and test analytic-brain dominant for the movement, unable to access the gestalt-brain to take over this activity once it is mastered. No matter how many times they cross-crawl, they keep learning it over and over, and it never becomes automatic and joyful.

## HOMOLATERAL OR INTEGRATED PATTERNS

When a person tests gestalt-brain dominant for crawling, his indicator muscle will test strong, suggesting that hemispheric integration is taking place. When a person tests analytic-brain dominant, his indicator muscle tests weak, indicating that hemispheric integration is failing to take place. We call the former people "heterolateral", "bi-lateral", or "laterally integrated", indicating that both sides can operate at one time, simultaneously. We call the latter people "homolateral" indicating that only one hemisphere is on at a given time. All those people who would have tested analytic-brained and weak on an indicator muscle when cross-crawling would not have benefitted from the crawling in the classroom or from the patterning for dyslexia as it has been traditionally prescribed. In fact, bilateral or cross-crawl movements might actually have further disorganized them! However, with Dennison Laterality Repatterning, whole body movement can quickly become the life-energizing tool it was meant to be!

"E-K Makes it Happen!"
LEFT-RIGHT HEMISPHERIC INTEGRATION
(to be used with E-K Worksheet)

## 1. GOAL FOR THE SESSION

Pick something your student would like to work on, and test him to
see if he is weak thinking about that subject. A session can focus on anything the student tests weak on, for example:  reading,
writing, spelling, math, driving, (or car passenger), playing a mu-
sical instrument, performing a sport, improving a relationship,
public speaking, singing, or whatever else presents itself. In
E-K, we balance for a function that the person wants to improve.

It is effective to obtain before and after samples of that task,
whenever possible.  For example, tape recorded oral reading is a
good idea, as most students will show a dramatic improvement in
reading during the first session!  You may also want to obtain a
sample of the student's writing and/or spelling, if written work
has proven difficult.  The more you can anchor change through
quick pretests and post tests, the more your student will realize
how much learning has taken place that is immediately applicable.

(Before beginning any procedure, you and your student do "brain
buttons" and "Cook's Hook-ups" and have a drink of water.)

## 2. LOCATION OF EXPRESSIVE (LANGUAGE) AND RECEPTIVE (GESTALT) HEMISPHERES

1.  To determine the hemispheric location of language, ask the
student to speak or count, then test both right and left deltoid
to see which one stays strong.  The expressive language/analytic
brain will be activating the opposite arm.  If the right arm holds
strong, and the left arm doesn't, then language is centered in the
left brain (the usual case).  Humming (in a monotone) or visualizing should strengthen the opposite (receptive/gestalt) brain, and
the other arm.  In some more difficult cases, there may be a deeper level or switching which keeps you from getting a clear answer
on hemispheric location.  If so, retest after the session.  Location of hemisheres is valuable information to know, but secondary
to the process of actually freeing up potential.

## 3. MENTAL FITNESS ENERGY

The Mental Fitness Energy is a number, on a scale of 1-40, for the actual energy level of the Thymus gland. This gland regulates the responsiveness of the brain and the distribution of energy within the system. To determine your student's "Mental Fitness Energy Level", test a strong indicator muscle in the clear. Retest as student touches Thymus with two fingers. A weak response shows Thymus energy could be increased. Now say, "This body has a Mental Fitness Energy of 40/40." If the muscle tests weak, explain that the body's higher wisdom didn't accept that statement as true, so the muscle could not resist. To find out what the true level is you must establish a baseline by dividing the figure in half (eg: 20/40, 10/40, or 5/40) until the muscle tests strong. Then count forward by increments of 10, 5, and then 1, until you find the highest number for which the person will test strong. When the true Mental Fitness Energy Level is determined, record it on the Worksheet in the "before" column.

## 4. EYES AND EARS IN THE CLEAR
## 4A. CROSSING THE MIDLINE FOR EYES

To test for "switching off" of eyes, test a strong indicator muscle in the clear. Now, using a pencil or penlight for a target, test the eyes in four positions: to the left, to the right, up, and down. This tests the awareness of each eye (and corresponding opposite brain) in each visual field. Is the brain registering from that visual field? Record findings on the worksheet.

## 4B. CROSSING THE MIDLINE FOR EARS

To test for "switching off" of the auditory field of each ear (and corresponding opposite brain), test for the ability to turn the head both ways. Note range of motion, as well as any tension in the neck. Test a strong indicator muscle in the clear. Now test with the head turned all the way to the left. This tests the proprioception of the neck muscles when responding to sound with the left ear, and right brain. Test again with head turned to the right. This tests the response to sound of the right ear and left brain. Record weaknesses on Worksheet.

## 5. EYES AND EARS AFTER TRACKING

5A. Test to see if coordination of the eyes crossing the "mid-field" or "midline", will cause "switching off". Challenge the student to track an object visually, back and forth across the midline for 20 repetitions, or until you see signs of stress. Your intention is to imitate the reading or writing experience. Object should be about 18" (normal reading distance for adults) or length of forearm, from the eyes. Emphasize the object's movement from student's left to right visual field, in imitation of reading. This is called the "pencil test" and is equivalent to reading for 1/2 hour. Retest the four positions and indicate "switching off" on the Worksheet.

5B. Retest the ears in both positions to see if the eye movement for tracking effects the auditory system. Record weaknesses on the worksheet.

## 6. CROSSING THE MIDLINE FOR WHOLE BODY MOVEMENT

To test for a homolateral preference, have the student cross crawl 10 or more times. This should make the indicator muscle strong. Now have her look at an X. This should also be strengthening, as it is the symbol for crossing the corpus collosum. Have the student homolateral crawl 10 or more times. This should make the indicator muscle weak, as it is a one-sided activity, and not a whole-brained one. Now have her look at 11. This should also be weak, as it is the homolateral, "one side at a time" symbol. (See page on Dennison Laterality Patterning for more information). Mark the Worksheet accordingly.

## 7. THE DENNISON LATERALITY TEST FOR DOMINANCE

The Dennison Laterality Test is used to determine if the dominance pattern is uniform, mixed, or blocked. (See sections on dominance)

## UNIFORM DOMINANCE

Laterality is uniform (sometimes called "normal") and, therefore not usually a problem for a person if he is right-handed, right-eyed, right-eared, and left-brained, with expressive (language/analytic) functions centered in the left cerebral hemisphere.

This person does not unsually have difficulty with reading skills. He would also be considered of uniform dominance if left-handed, left-eyed, and left-eared, and right-language-brained. (However, in this case he might have reading difficulty if he switches off his dominant left language eye when leading with the right eye in order to follow the reading line from left to right.

"CROSS" OR MIXED DOMINANCE

Directionality and perceptual problems most often develop when there is "mixed" or "cross" dominance. This confusion often results from an inner confusion, in the homolateral state, between dominant hand controlled by one hemisphere and dominant eye or ear controlled by the other.

BLOCKED DOMINANCE

Blocked dominance, an unusual situation, can also result in energy blockages, as this pattern is highly stressful. In the blocked pattern, the student is all right-sided and right-brained as well, or all left-sided and left-brained. The dominant eye, ear and hand all require the control of the non-dominant brain. The dominant hemisphere (and personality), especially in the homolateral state, is difficult to access.

TESTING FOR DOMINANT EYE
To determine the dominant eye, have student look through a peek-hole the size of a quarter in paper held in his two outstretched hands. Have him look at your nose from a distance of ten feet. You will see him choose his dominant eye unconsciously as he aims the paper. (Your student may choose the eye which is "task dominant" for reading if you test at too close a distance).

TESTING FOR THE DOMINANT EAR
To determine the dominant ear, test a strong indicator muscle in the clear. Have your student touch two fingers of one hand to his earlobe. Say, "This arm is weak," while retesting the muscle. Test again with fingers on the other earlobe, repeating the suggestion. The dominant ear will not take the false suggestion; the non-dominant ear will.

TESTING FOR THE DOMINANT BRAIN

To test for the dominant brain, test as for the ear, placing the two fingers now against the right or left temples.

EVALUATION: After making E-K corrections, retest as much as posible. Is the Mental Fitness Energy now 40/40? Do eye and ear coordination exercises test strong instead of weak? Are all muscles now strong on cross-crawl and the X? Do they all test weak on homolateral crawl and the 11? Does student test strong now when thinking of his goal? Is reading much easier and does it sound full of energy? Is phrasing more fluid, breathing more natural, and speech more communicative? A comparison of the before and after taped readings will speak for itself. Share with your student all of his strengths. Anchor all tasks with a strong muscle test and positive responses.

For whatever you focused the session, be it reading, writing, spelling, posture, or other dimensions of growth, always discuss the before and after experience as that is a way of reinforcing the positive changes.

Teacher, congratulations! You have succeeded in guiding your student to a higher level of integration.

Student, congratulations! You have succeeded in opening yourself to positive life changes.


INTERPRETATION-     "Mind that Matters"

The Dennison Laterality Test for Dominance provides extremely valuable information to be interpreted by the skilled E-K Consultant.

Recent brain research suggests that up to 80% of the population has "overlap" of brain function. This means that only 20% are really what we have defined as "uniform". As a result, people do not always use the most efficient strategies available to them. E-K testing often shows unusual "overlap" patterns (such as language and gestalt both in the same hemisphere) in the initial visit. After E-K repatterning, people learn strategies which involve more of the whole brain, and more hemispheric specialization, instead of both sides of the brain doing the same job.

As a E-K Consultant, you can help your student to understand his inefficient strategies better by explaining his dominance profile to him, and by showing him where he has been switching off for specific tasks.

# EDU-KINESTHETICS WORKSHEET FOR
## LEFT/RIGHT HEMISPHERIC INTEGRATION

Name_____ Age_____ Date_____ Phone_____

School_____ Grade_____ Teacher_____

1. GOAL_____

2. HEMISPHERIC LOCATION OF FUNCTIONS  (Circle one)

   Expressive (Analytic-language-try)  left   right   overlap

   Receptive (Gestalt-visual-reflex)  left   right   overlap

|  | BEFORE CORRECTION | AFTER CORRECTION |
|---|---|---|
| 3. MENTAL FITNESS ENERGY LEVEL | /40 | /40 |
| 4.   EYES AND EARS IN THE CLEAR | | |
| 4A. Eyes, crossing midline (Circle if off) | r l up down | r l up down |
| 4B. Ears, crossing midline (Circle if off) | right left | right left |
| 5.   EYES AND EARS AFTER TRACKING OR READING | | |
| 5A. Eyes, crossing midline (Circle if off) | r l up down | r l up down |
| 5B. Ears, crossing midline (Circle if off) | right left | right left |
| 6.   CROSSING THE MIDLINE FOR WHOLE BODY MOVEMENT | | |
| Cross-crawl    (Circle bi-hemispheric response) | on      off | on      off |
| Homolateral crawl | on      off | on      off |
| X | on      off | on      off |
| 11 | on      off | on      off |

7. DENNISON LATERALITY TEST  (Circle if dominant)

| | | | |
|---|---|---|---|
| Hand | right | left | ambidexterous |
| Eye | right | left | |
| Ear | right | left | balanced |
| BRAIN | right | left | integrated |

From the above results, which one of three dominance profiles is indicated?

___Uniform (Reader)   ___Mixed or cross   ___Blocked

45

# E-K DIMENSION INDICATORS
## "Inner energy reflects outer energy"

## INTRODUCTION TO THE THREE E-K DIMENSIONS

E-K works with the three dimensions of the brain/body system.
These are the laterality dimension (left and right body and brain
hemispheres), the centering dimension (top and bottom body and
brain), and the back/front dimension (back body and brain to front
body and frontal lobes). How do these three dimensions apply to
one's ability to learn and express herself or himself?

## LATERALITY DIMENSION

The first of these three dimensions, emphasized especially in this
Basic II Workshop, is the laterality dimension. This is the dimension related to the left and right hemisheres of the brain and the
left and right sides of the body. This dimension concerns the a-
bility to work in the midfield and to cross the midline. It is affected by homolateral behavior, lateral dominance patterns, trans-
position of hemispheres, and "switching off" of eyes and ears.

## EFFECT OF LATERALITY ON READING SKILLS

When Johnny reads, his receptive hemisphere may help him to blend
phonemes into recognizable syllables, perceive visual information,
maintain a cohesive story line, enjoy the humor or other emotional
content, draw upon meaning from past associations, and understand
metaphor. At the same time, his expressive hemisphere helps him
decode the written words into phonemes, derive abstract meaning
from complex relationships among word concepts and syntax, and understand what he reads in terms of himself and his own experiences.

## EFFECT OF READING SKILLS ON LATERALITY

However, this can happen for Johnny only if he has completed successfully some important developmental stages that allow him to
function with both hemispheres on together for eyes, ears, and

46

whole body movement for the complex near-point activity of reading across the midline. For many children entering school, these developmental processes are not complete, and reading and writing activities actually cause "switching off" of eyes and/or ears, and, therefore, the brain, as a compensatory mechanism to "succeed" at academic skills.

E-K DIMENSION INDICATORS- "fig leafs"

To quickly determine if someone is not functioning at his potential for the laterality dimension, the E-K Consultant can test the Supraspinatus muscle we call the "fig leaf" because of the position of the arms and hands for the muscle test. The student holds his arms about one foot in front of him with his hands pointed toward the "fig leaf" or pubic bone area. The student is instructed to "hold" as you push on the arm toward the "fig leaf". If the arm goes down, the student is experiencing some difficulty in the laterality dimension.

When the laterality dimension is blocked, the student may need a corrective E-K session or he may need to do some "midline movements" and/or some "energy exercises" from Brain Gym to switch himself back on.

CENTERING DIMENSION

To be centered means to have a sense of balance and overall whole-body coordination. To be centered means you experience a sense of "groundedness" and an integrity of the upper and lower halves of the body as they work together. The laterality dimension depends upon how well centered and balanced you are when you do activities involving the crossing of the midline.

When Erin reads, her level of centering affects her ability to be organized as she reads. It keeps her "centered" on the midfield of the page, aware of her body comfort and her breathing, and keeps her voice full and strong. It keeps her "centered" in her thinking, internalizing the information in terms of her own life experiences as she reads.

E-K DIMENSION INDICATORS- "swimmers"

To quickly determine if someone is "uncentered" and in need of E-K
to improve her performance, test the pectoralis major clavicular
or "swimmer" muscles. The student holds her arms straight out in
front of her, hands turned out, as if she was swimming. You push
the arm down and out, away from her midline. If the arm goes down
this means that the student is "uncentered" for some reason and
will not be able to perform at her best. She may need an E-K corrective session or she may need to do some "deepening attitudes"
and/or "energy exercises" from Brain Gym.

BACK/FRONT DIMENSION

Back/Front Dimension has to do with concentration, focus, and the
ability to retrieve information from the back of the brain and to
bring it forward to the frontal lobes for analysis and reflection.
The laterality dimension depends upon the integrity of the back/
front dimension for the ability to comprehend one's own experience
and to concentrate upon the task at hand.

When Thomas reads, his level of back/front integration affects his
ability to relate appropriately to the information. If he is over-
focused, he gets so absorbed in the material that he loses track
of everything else around him. He cannot seem to "see the forest
for the trees" and is unable to keep a perspective about what he
reads - taking it all too personally. If he is underfocused, he
is too "held back" and seems to have a wall between his prior experiences and "old information" and this new input. He has difficulty seeing the relevance of reading to his life. He cannot concentrate or give his full attention to the task at hand. He is unable to anticipate, predict or think ahead of himself. He cannot
comprehend or paraphrase into his own words. He does not bring any
"life" or energy to what he is doing.

E-K DIMENSION INDICATORS- "Penguins"

A quick method to determine if your student is able to focus in
the back/front dimension is to test the latissimus dorsi or "penguin" muscle. Have the student hold his arms at his sides with

the hands turned, palms out, like a penguin while testing. The
student holds his arm as if "glued" to his side while you attempt
to pull the arm away from the body. If the muscle is "switched
off", the student will not be able to do his best work because
there is not sufficient back/front energy flow. The student may
need E-K corrective measures or he may need to do some "lengthening exercises" and/or some "energy exercises" from Brain Gym to
switch himself on.

# E-K CORRECTION PROCEDURES
## def: "to bring to life: to bring to consciousness"

## DENNISON LATERALITY REPATTERNING

1. TESTING
   A. Test a strong indicator muscle in the clear.
   B. Have the student cross-crawl, touching hand to opposite knee, for 10-20 repetitions. (Each side once is a full repetition.)
   C. Test the indicator muscle. Note: Is it strong or weak? If it is weak, the student may be homolateral. Confirm the finding with the remaining tests.
   D. Have the student homolateral crawl, touching hand to the same knee, for 10-20 repetitions.
   E. Test the indicator muscle. Note: Is it strong or weak? If it is strong, the student is homolateral and needs repatterning.
   F. Have the student look at an X. If X weakens the indicator muscle, the student is homolateral.
   G. Have the student look at two parallel vertical lines, II. If this strengthens the indicator muscle, the student is homolateral.

2. REPATTERNING

   A. Muscle test the student to see if he/she is ready for further integration. If so, proceed. If not, wait for a more appropriate time.
   B. Have the student cross-crawl, as in number 1A above, with eyes purposefully turned to access the reflex brain. (Usually up to the left, as reflex is on the right side of the brain for most people).
   C. Retest the indicator muscle, noting that it is now strong on cross-crawl; not weak as it was previously. If it is still weak, have your student cross-crawl wih his eyes up to the right instead. Repeat the muscle test. It should now be strong.

50

D. Have the student homolateral crawl, as in number 1D above, with eyes turned to access the analytic brain. (Down to the right, if 2B was eyes up left indicating that the analytic brain is on the left side.)
E. Retest the indicator muscle, noting that it is now weak on this activity; not strong. If it is not weak, do more repetitions, or continue with eyes down to the left, instead of right.

3. INTEGRATION

A. Have student clasp his/her two hands together to symbolically integrate the two brain hemispheres "feeling the two brains working together."
B. Have the student cross-crawl with eyes looking in all directions.
C. Retest the indicator muscle. It should be strong, no matter where the student points his/her eyes.
D. Have the student homolateral crawl with eyes looking in all directions.
E. Retest the indicator muscle. It should be weak, no matter where the student points his/her eyes.
F. Retest looking at the X. The indicator muscle should now be strong.
G. Retest looking at the II. The indicator muscle should now be weak.
H. Discuss any changes the student is experiencing. This has been a moment of rebirth for thousands of people.

Dennison Laterality Repatterning is effective because it works in accord with Nature as she intended us to learn. This repatterning gives people permission to cross the midline, restoring the natural process of the infant to trust, to let go of conscious control, and to access the right-brain for movement. Dennison Laterality Repatterning seems simple, yet requires instruction and understanding to go from step to step. If you have not experienced it yet, ask an E-K instructor to repattern you. If you know the technique, repattern as many people as you can find.

Dennison Laterality Repatterning is not suggested as a panacea for all our ills. As one of the first steps of any sound educational or health maintenance program, it is providing results for people who have failed to find help elsewhere. It is literally true, as many are learning, that we must crawl before we walk!

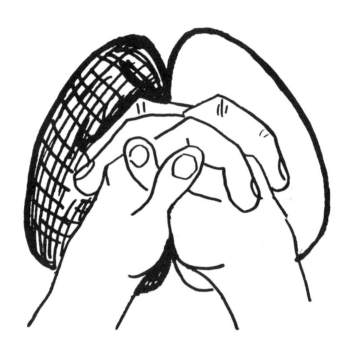

HOMOLATERAL MUSCLE CORRECTION

Note: This homolateral muscle correction is performed as a ritual. A step by step suggested procedure is presented here; however, individual circumstances may necessitate flexibility. It is
essential for the "whole" picture to always be present in the mind
of the student- that cross crawl should make all the muscle systems strong and that homolateral crawl should make all the muscle
systems weak. Help your student to enjoy the experience of making
this a reality.

IN PREPARATION

1. Establish that homolateral muscle correction is the next thing
   to work on.

2. "This body has 5 or more homolateral muscles." (Determine the
   exact number.)

3. "These muscles are above the waist; below the waist; on the
   front of the body;...on the back." (Determine general loca-
   tions.)

IDENTIFICATION

4. Have student cross crawl on his/her back touching hand to knee
   for 10-20 repetitions.

5. Test the Touch for Health muscles, using 14 or more indicator
   muscles, noting which muscles are weak after cross crawl.
   These may be homolateral.

6. "We have identified enough homolateral muscles." (Some of the
   weak muscles may not be homolateral muscles, but all homolateral muscles will be weak.)

7. Have student homolateral crawl on his/her back, touching hand to knee on the same side of the body, for 10-20 repetitions.

8. Retest the indicator muscles, using Touch for Health tests, as before. Note any muscles that were previously weak that are now strong. (All muscles should be weak on homolateral crawl, as this is a "one brain at a time" state.)

9. Any muscle that was weak on cross crawl and strong on homolateral crawl is a homolateral muscle.

10. "We have identified the homolateral muscles...this body is ready to integrate these muscles at a deeper level..."

REPATTERNING FOR X; CROSS CRAWL

1. "This body needs to cross crawl (test) eyes up to the left (test) 10 or more times (determine number by testing - use positive points if more than 50 repetitions).

2. Have student cross crawl effortlessly like a little child, while activating gestalt brain.You do the counting. Instruct him to hum if you think he might be counting or "trying too hard".

3. Retest the previously homolateral muscles. They should now be strong.

REPATTERNING FOR II; HOMOLATERAL CRAWL

4. "This body needs to homolateral crawl (test) eyes down to the right (test) 10 or more times" (as before).

5. Have student homolateral crawl consciously, activating the analytic centers of the brain by counting as he moves.

6. Retest the previously homolateral muscles. They should now all test weak.

INTEGRATION

7. "This body is ready for the integration metaphor." (test) Have the student imagine that he holds his 2 hemispheres in his hands. He slowly brings them together, clasping his hands and intertwining his fingers. You may suggest that he "feel" the two hemispheres working together in harmony.

ANCHORING FOR X; CROSS CRAWL

8. Now have your student cross crawl, looking in all directions of the clock.

9. Anchor with as many muscles as you feel are appropriate - that his whole body is now strong on cross crawl. Most people are stronger than ever at this point, as the integrated strength is more effortless than one-brained strength!

ANCHORING FOR II; HOMOLATERAL CRAWL

10. Have him homolateral crawl, eyes looking in all directions.

11. Anchor again; this time all muscles should be weak.

12. Explain that this "one brain at a time state" is now his low gear, allowing him to shut down and really "focus in" consciously when he needs to.

13. Now teach the power of "mind over matter"! Have him think of an X. All his muscles will be strong, with an integrated strength!

14. Have him roll off the table and walk around, sharing any changes he experiences in his mind and body.

# THE LAZY 8
"We are each at the center of a personal Universe"


## INFINITY SIGN

The lazy 8, or infinity sign, has been used in special education
and vision training for many years, because it gets results.  The
lazy 8 has been validated by E-K muscle testing.  The lazy 8 works
successfully because it enables the student to cross the midline
with a continuous line, thus preventing him or her from switching
off the right brain energy flow.  The lazy 8 is a symbol which
"centers" people temporarily, thus opening the nervous system to
more energy while its effects last.  The effect is to temporarily
balance the student so that integrated learning can be accomplished and stored.

Several innovations have been developed by our E-K research using
the lazy 8.  These techniques make the lazy 8 that much more effective.

In Edu-Kinesthetics we recognize that all learning is task specific.  In human behavior, we cannot depend upon "transfer" from one
learning situation to another.  As you develop your relationship
with your student, do lazy 8's on all subjects, and aspects of subjects, which need better integration.  The lazy 8 is a tool for per-
manently integrate those activities which had, beforehand, been
done in a homolateral manner.

## LAZY 8 ON THE CHALKBOARD

Draw a lazy 8 on the board, as large as the student can reach com-
fortably.  The student traces the lazy 8, counterclockwise to the
left first, first with one hand, then the other, and then with both
hands together.  Repeat until it is effortless and requires no conscious thought.  This switches on the eye-hand coordination for
visually crossing the midline.  Variations can be done on all different surfaces and textures. Tracking and other eye exercises are
only to be done after this lazy 8 is completed and both eyes test
as "switched on".

LAZY 8 FOR WRITING

In order to print, and later to write, the energy must flow as one forms, first lines into letters, and, then, letters into words. The lower case letters are formed by integrating the "counterclockwise" and "clockwise" circles of the lazy 8 with a vertical line at the center. Letters activating the left eye and right brain begin at the center and move in a counterclockwise circle, up and overhand, and end at the midline. Letters activating the right eye and left brain begin at the midline on the downstroke (if there is one) and move clockwise. (For more on 8's for writing, see Switching On, chapter 9.)

THE ELEPHANT 8 FOR EARS

The student draws the lazy 8 against a fixed plane on the horizon with an imaginary elephant's trunk or paintbrush extending from his outstretched arm. The head and shoulder are locked. The whole body draws the figure, without moving the head, neck, or shoulders separately. Make sure the knees bend and the body sways rhythmically from side to side. This switches on the proprioception in the neck and improves listening, speaking, and memory skills, previously done with the neck blocked and switched off.

# BRAIN GYM
"A few minutes of doing something correctly can
transform a lifetime of doing it incorrectly."


## MIDLINE MOVEMENTS

1. Cross Crawl, "Skip-a-Cross", and Cross Crawl dancing (eg.
   waltz, charleston, rhumba)

   There are many variations.  For the E-K correction procedures,
   Dennison Laterality Repatterning and Homolateral Muscle Correction, the hands must touch the opposite knees and the direction
   of the eyes is important.  For "brain gym" we just have fun,
   moving the arms and legs in all positions and moving the eyes
   in all directions. See Switching On and E-K For Kids for more
   ideas.

2. Cross Crawl Sit-ups
   For strengthening the abdominals and back muscles: the best
   way to do sit-ups is to cross crawl, on the back, bicycle
   style, touching elbow to opposite knee.

3. Neck Rolls
   Roll the neck gently three times in each direction, breathing
   slowly and letting go of any tension experienced in your body.
   A visualization that your head is separate and unattached to
   the body is often helpful.

4. Belly Breathing
   This exercise is done by those who need to learn to breathe into the abdominal area.  Place a book on the belly and make it
   rise on inhalation.  Experience the breath expanding the rib
   cage in the front, the sides and the back and lengthening the
   torso up into the neck area and down into the abdomen.  Repeat
   three times.

5. The Cobra
   The cobra is a yoga posture. Lying on your stomach, with fingers under the shoulders pointed toward the center of the body, become a cobra. Lift first the eyes, then head, then back, allowing energy, not strength, to move you up, without disturbing the lower half of the body. Avoid any shoulder activation or effort in the arms.

6. The Rocker
   The rocker stimulates the circulation of cerebrospinal fluid by loosening and flexing the sacrum. Sit on a padded surface with the knees raised, heels touching the surface. Grasp the knees with both hands and lean the upper body backward until both arms are straight and your weight is on the sacrum (triangular bone between the hip bones). Rock backward holding on to the knees so that the feet are lifted from the surface, EXHALING DEEPLY as you rock backward, and INHALING as you rock forward. A variation is to rock from side to side, leaning back on the hands, gently massaging the sacrum.

7. Figure 8's for eyes
   Figure 8's should be done before new visual activities, such as reading, driving, viewing films etc. Figure 8's are always done overhand as taught in this manual. Vary the texture for different tactile experiences.

8. The Elephant
   The elephant should be done before new auditory or language experiences. Do it facing the sky, the horizon, with each side of the body. Be aware of changes in the neck.

9. Figure 8's for writing
   Figure 8's for writing should be done before written work. Pay special attention to letters which have been or continue to be difficult. Only "lowercase" letters should be done. You may separate the letters into two groups, doing all the gestalt-activating ones first (eg: a, c, d, e, f, g, o, q, s) and finish with the language-activating letters.

LENGTHENING EXERCISES

10. The Owl

This is an extension exercise for the upper trapezius muscle
which affects the flow of cerebrospinal fluid. Grasp and
squeeze the right upper trapezius with the left hand as firmly
as you can. Turn the head slowly, as far as you can in each
direction, looking back, over the shoulders, like an owl. Drop
your chin onto your chest and lengthen the back neck extensors.
Repeat three times, then change sides.

11. Arm Extension

This exercise releases tension in the shoulders and arms. Hold
one arm against the side of the head with the other hand. Activate the arm isometrically in all directions, exhaling as
you exert the muscle.

12. Calf Extension

This exercise releases tension in the leg muscles. In the
standing position, place both hands on a table or wall. Extending one leg directly behind you with heel touching the floor,
lean forward placing weight on the bent front leg. Feel the
lengthening in the rear calf. EXHALE and HOLD for five seconds. Repeat three times with each leg.

13. Hamstring Extension

Student sits on the side of a sturdy table so that one leg is
on the floor and the other leg is flat on the table in front
of him, with the toe pointed up. He should grasp the under
side of the table for support and lean forward, EXHALING for
ten seconds, keeping the leg absolutely straight, until tightness (not pain) is experienced in the back of the leg and/or
knee. The intention is to lift the table, sandwiching the
leg, rather than pushing the back down. No tension must be
experienced in the lower back. Alternate three repetitions
with each leg.

14. Psoas Extension

With hands on hips, extend leg behind you, with foot turned
out to the side. Lunge forward, bending the front knee until
you feels tightness (not pain) in the psoas (pelvis) area. Repeat three times with each leg.

ENERGY EXERCISES

15. Brain Buttons
   Massage vigorously the Kidney 27 areas (the soft spots under the clavicle) for thirty seconds, while holding the navel.

16. Thinking Cap
   Unfold the ears, from top to bottom, three times each.

17. Earth Buttons
   For the ability to look down and to be better "grounded" hold the pubic bone and spot below the lower lip for thirty seconds or until you feel a pulse.

18  Space Buttons
   For the ability to look up and to be more open to the information around you, hold the tail bone and spot above the upper lip for thirty seconds or until you feel a pulse.

19. Balance Buttons
   For the ability to stay more centered, hold the mastoid process, GB 20, (just behind the ear) on each side while holding the navel with the other hand.  Hold each side for thirty seconds or until you feel a pulse.

20. Yawn
   Pretend to yawn gently, even making the sound, until real yawns are easy, automatic and not forced or stifled. This relaxes the jaw and neck.


DEEPENING ATTITUDES

21. Positive Points
   See Switching On, and E-K For Kids.

22. Cooks-Hook-ups
   See E-K For Kids

# COOK'S HOOK-UPS
## "Intend to Nurture"

PHASE I

PHASE II

PHASE I

A. Sitting in a comfortable chair, cross left leg over right knee.
   (exception taught in class)
B. Hold left ankle with right hand.
C. Hold the "ball" of left foot with left hand as illustrated.
D. Relax and breathe deeply with tongue against roof of mouth on
   inhale and behind bottom teeth on exhale.
   HOLD THE POSTURE FOR AT LEAST ONE MINUTE!

PHASE 2

A. Sitting with both feet on he floor, touch the fingers of one
   hand against the fingers of the other.
B. Continue to breathe deeply, as before.
   HOLD FOR AT LEAST ONE MINUTE!

# POSITIVE POINTS
## "Energy Follows Intention"

PURPOSE
To transmute fear into love. To see the positive side of all situations. To have more integrated emotional involvement.

APPLICATIONS
To integrate all types of mental and emotional distress: grief,
fear, anger, frustration, nightmares, and any real or imagined
stress which makes one weak.

To rewrite the past (replay old negative experiences).

To plan the future (image and rehearse future scenarios which
would ordinarily cause worry and, instead, enjoy the challenge by
releasing anticipated stress.

To eliminate conditioned responses to specific people and environmental factors (imagining the person's face or the environmental
factor until the indicator muscle tests strong).

PROCEDURE
1. Test a strong indicator muscle. Since stress or negative
   thinking "uncenters" people, the best muscle to use is the
   "swimmer" or pectoralis major clavicular.

2. Have the student think of what she perceives as her "problem"
   instead of her "challenge".

3. Retest the indicator muscle. The muscle will test weak if she
   is uncentered.

4. Hold the Positive Points lightly (usually
   for 20 to 30 seconds) where indicated in
   the illustration while the student thinks
   about the same "problem" again. Hold with
   just enough pressure to pull the skin taut
   between the two points.

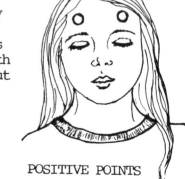

5. Retest the indicator muscle. The muscle
   will be strong when the process is complete. If still weak, number 4 until the
   indicator muscle is strong.

POSITIVE POINTS

BEHAVIOR PATTERNS THAT MAY INDICATE LACK OF INTEGRATION

This list of behaviors was compiled to help the E-K Consultant to set goals and to notice changes after working with E-K in a family situation. E-K creates changes in behavior when people are ready to release old patterns. It is recommended that no special attention be called to these behaviors as listed. All children exhibit one or more of these behaviors at a given time. It is important to separate the occasional from the persistent, and to avoid concern about isolated incidents or brief developmental deviations.

INFANCY
Trouble with nursing, sucking, or digesting.
Resistance to or excessive demand for cuddling, and body contact.
Lack of response or excessive response to sound.
Inability to hold head upright.
Trouble following movements with the eyes.
Absence of creeping and crawling.
Delay in or premature sitting, standing or walking.
Delay in learning to talk.

PRE-SCHOOL YEARS
Excessive crying; disturbed sleep.
Poor sense of rhythm; uneven walk.
Fear of swings and slides.
Frequent falls and a tendency to bump into things.
Tendency to be fearless, climbing counters and roofs with no concern.
Excessive craving for sugar and poor eating habits.
Inability to follow directions.
Impulsive and uncontrolled behavior.
Purposeless hyperactivity.
Unusual quietness and lethargy.
Constant interrupting and persistent chattering.
Excessive repetition in speaking, questioning, and playing.
Tendency to become more upset with others than when alone.
Language problems as evidenced by delayed talking and confused or garbled speech.

## SCHOOL YEARS

Difficulty with skipping, hopping, and jumping.

Clumsiness and awkwardness in throwing and catching a ball.

Excessive activity which seems purposeless, restless, and undirected.

Unusual inactivity characterized by day-dreaming and inner distraction.

Trouble with game playing and following group rules.

Excessive gullibility.

Emotional instability; explosions for no apparent reason.

Tendency to be extremely literal or humorless.

Difficulty cutting with scissors and coloring inside lines.

Inability to tie shoe laces, close buttons, or use hands efficiently.

Trouble in matching shapes and sizes: squares, circles, triangles.

Confusion in discrimination of letters, numbers, and words: "b" and d", "was" and "saw", "6" and "9".

Poor understanding of the difference between up and down, in and out, right and left, front and back.

Confused sense of time and distance.

Good verbal abilities, but inability to read and write.

Difficulty in expressing ideas.

Mechanical reading without comprehension.

Very poor or illegible handwriting.

Erratic school work.

Extremely uneven performance in testing; scoring high in some areas, and way below normal in others.

RECOGNIZING SWITCHED OFF BEHAVIORS
"I'm hiding, I'm hiding,
And no one knows where,
For all they can see is my
Toes and my hair."
(from the poem "Hiding" by Dorothy Aldis)


## CLUES TO BLOCKED POTENTIALS

Most parents "know" that potential learning disabilities exist
long before they manifest at school. The tendency is to overlook
these suspicions, however, in hopes that children will "magically"
outgrow these behaviors with time. Educators, as well, often believe that learning problems will solve themselves when the child
reaches an age when she is more "ready" to learn.

Educational Kinesiology is a tool to take the guesswork and opin-
ion out of education and childrearing. It is now possible to recognize the early signs of learning problems so that help can be pro-
vided before "failure" affects the child's self-concept about her
ability to learn at school.

In Educational Kinesiology the physical body and its ability to
move naturally and efficiently is the best clue to unblocked learning potential. By observing a child's compensatory behaviors while
at play or when learning a new skill, the E-K Consultant can quickly recognize "switched off" patterns for processing information.

Included here are several behavior profiles, describing how selected students were observed to compensate for their "switched off"
dominance pattern. Once recognized and analyzed, corrections can
be made to "switch on" the student so that neither hemisphere pre-
dominates, both working together in a more integrated fashion. Following the corrections, Brain Gym exercises reinforce the changes
and recommendations can be made to build on the strengths of the
individual's strategy for learning.

SELECTED BEHAVIOR PROFILES

1. 7-year-old Nathan turns sideways when drawing, cutting, or writing. He is always sprawling sideways, one way or the other, unable to sit straight in his chair.

This child is avoiding his natural "midline" working area where the visual fields overlap naturally, thus teaching himself to process with one brain hemisphere only. When he is "trying" he must switch off his "receptive" brain which sees the whole picture. This is the most common pattern exhibited by people with learning problems.

DOMINANCE PROFILE: Cross dominant; Right(gestalt)-brain, right-hand, left-eye, left ear.

CORRECTION: Dennison Laterality Repatterning, Figure 8's for eyes, elephant 8 for ears.

BRAIN GYM: cross crawl, brain buttons, large bi-lateral finger painting. Also recommended were more "gestalt" activities: whole body play, tumbling, dance.

2. When Santia, age 8, gets absorbed in her work she stands up to draw, cut or write. She works seriously and carefully; easily frustrated by what she judges as mistakes. Santia is very skilled at drawing and small motor tasks. She is a very quiet child, not seeming to be very interested in talking or socializing with others.

This child may be unable to focus her eyes in the reading position and may have blurred or double vision. By looking down at her work she may be compensating to avoid visual confusion such as switching off the visual information to one of the brain hemispheres.

DOMINANCE PROFILE: Blocked dominant; right(language)-brain(transposed hemispheres), right-eye, right ear, ambidexterous, but eats and writes with right hand.

CORRECTION: Homolateral Muscle Correction, Figure 8's for writing.

BRAIN GYM: cross crawl, brain buttons, earth buttons, space buttons, balance buttons. After discussion about Santia's dominance pattern with her parents, freestyle dramatic play, dance, and other creative expression activities were recommended to give her the opportunity to use the dominant language brain. Until she is able to achieve greater whole body-brain integration, further mastery of small motor skills with her right hand may only tend to block language/expressive development.

3. Scott is 12. He runs with his eyes down and his feet turned in. Scott began wearing glasses for reading about three years ago. He does well in school, but seems to work harder than is necessary to make the grade and never seems to enjoy himself.

This child is overfocusing and, later, may be unable to relax his eyes and body to get the full perspective on what he is doing. This behavior often results in nearsightedness or other visual compensations. This child is switching off the receptive brain when he tries or must alternate from hemisphere to hemisphere in homoateral fashion. Although learning handicapped by his style of processing, children like Scott are often overachievers, functioning as "good" students.

DOMINANCE PROFILE: Uniform; Left(language)-brain, right-hand, right-eye, right ear.

CORRECTION: Positive Points, Dennison Laterality Repatterning.

BRAIN GYM: cross-crawl, belly breathing, neck rolls, the owl. Taught to muscle test for books which are "fun" to be read at home.

4. Laura, at age 5, avoids turning her head and has frequent spills and accidents. She does not hold her head up straight, tipping her head up or to the side, as though the neck muscles are weak.

Laura tests that she is switching off her gestalt eye, therefore lacking a development of depth perception and awareness. She may have a "lazy eye" or a functional "lazy eye" which only switches off in certain circumstances.

DOMINANCE PROFILE: Uniform; left(language)-brain, right-hand, right-eye, right-ear.

CORRECTION: Dennison Laterality Repatterning, Homolateral muscle correction, figure 8's for eyes.

BRAIN GYM: cross crawl, calf extension, the rocker, the elephant. She was encouraged to do more spatial play, with large blocks. Swinging was recommended to help her coordination and visual awareness.


5. Jerry, age 11, avoids eye contact when listening or speaking and limits the turning of his head in these situations. This child is switching off his ears as indicated by the lack of responsiveness in the neck to the sounds of language. Jerry is unable to remember directions and follow them. He appears to daydream, preferring music and nonverbal sounds over speech. This child does not use his body to communicate and needs to develop the relationship between movement and language. He needs to develop the ability to switch on both ears simultaneously in order to process serial auditory information in his short-term memory.

DOMINANCE PROFILE: Cross Dominance; Right(gestalt)-brain, right-hand, right eye, left ear.

CORRECTION: Cook's Hook-ups, Dennison Laterality Repatterning, The Elephant 8 for ears.

BRAIN GYM: Cross crawl, thinking cap, neck rolls. Jerry was encouraged to read, sing, and talk into his tape recorder and to participate in the reading and writing of poetry for extra credit at school.

6. Justin, age 9, holds stress in the mouth, tongue, and neck when cutting, drawing, or writing and he tires easily.

This child has hand-eye coordination problems which cause switching off of one eye and brain when working in the midline area.

DOMINANCE PROFILE: Uniform; Right(gestalt)-brain, left-hand, left-eye, left-ear. (Note: switches off his dominant left, gestalt, eye.)

CORRECTION: Brain Buttons, Dennison Laterality Repatterning, Figure 8's for writing.

BRAIN GYM: cross crawl, balance buttons, earth buttons, space buttons. He was encouraged to develop his gestalt potential more through soccer, manual construction, and manipulative math.

7. Sean, age 16, exhibits breathing problems such as wheezing, gasping, or shortness of breath when doing near point work. A successful athelete, his failure to achieve better than average grades is causing increasing stress.

This child is switching off his brain for breathing, thus blocking sufficient energy to the brain for bi-hemispheric learning.

DOMINANCE PROFILE: Cross Dominant; right(gestalt)-brain, left-hand, right eye, right ear. (Note: Switching off left gestalt eye and ear for fine motor skills.)

CORRECTION: Cook's Hook-ups, Homolateral Muscle Correction.

BRAIN GYM: cross crawl, belly breathing, hamstring extension.

8. Renee is 15. She stands with knees locked and walks with feet turned out. Renee is unable to focus or concentrate or give her full attention to what she is doing. This type of switching off involves inhibition of the expressive brain, which explains why she appears uninterested and doesn't seem to care about any-thing.

DOMINANCE PROFILE: Cross dominant; Right(gestalt)-brain, left-hand, right-eye, right-ear. (Note: switching off right auditory/language eye and ear.)

CORRECTION: Cook's Hook-ups, Brain buttons, homolateral Muscle correction, figure 8's for eyes, writing.

BRAIN GYM: cross crawl, extension for shoulders/arms, calves, and the owl. Renee needed some encouragement to pursue her interest in jazz dancing.

9. Arthur, age 29, tilts his head to one side or seems to always strain the neck forward. He complains of tension headaches, shoulder pain, and some "ringing" in the ears. He finds near point work very stressful. He is a chronic smoker, unable to cut down because of stress.

Arthur is switching off visually in all four directions due to weak or undeveloped neck muscles. This often leads to visual and/or to auditory perception problems. The stress of compensating often leads people to rely on unnatural methods to function at all.

DOMINANCE PROFILE: Uniform (transposed); left(gestalt)-brain, right-hand, right-eye, right-ear.

CORRECTION: Positive points, brain buttons, homolateral muscle correction, The Elephant for ears.

BRAIN GYM: cross crawl, neck rolls, the cobra, the owl

10. Robin at age 5 appears clumsy. She walked early, yet cannot skip or ride a bicycle, avoiding movement and physical activities.

This child did not develop hemispheric integration during the creeping and crawling stage of development. This child is only able to function with one hemisphere at one time, thinking and moving remaining separate functions. The movements across the midline when learning to read and write may prove difficult or impossible.

<u>DOMINANCE PROFILE</u>: Cross dominant; Left(gestalt)-brain transposed, Left-handed, right-eyed, left-eared.

CORRECTION: Brain buttons, Dennison Laterality Repatterning, Figure 8's for eyes.

BRAIN GYM: cross crawl, bi-lateral drawing, balance buttons. It was suggested to her parents that they do whole body play with Robin. Fingerpainting, block building, swinging are all encouraged. Robin should not be frustrated with reading at this point.


11. Tracy, at age 13, just recently began to experience stress at school. She is unable to concentrate on her studies, prefer-ring to listen to loud music. She needs to be eating cook-ies or pop when she does do homework and "creates confusion around herself" (explains her mother) in order to complete anything.

This child is switching off her eyes and ears in all directions. She tests strong on both X and II indicating an inability to relax her body when she needs to focus.

<u>DOMINANCE PROFILE</u>: Cross dominance; Left(language)-brain, right-hand, left-eye, left ear.

CORRECTION: Cook's Hook-ups, Dennison Laterality Repatterning.

BRAIN GYM: Cook's Hook-ups, cross crawl, balance buttons, thinking cap. She was encouraged to create a daily play time for herself which would involve pleasurable movement.


12. Charles, age 6, appears unable to sit still or to concentrate more than 2 minutes on anything. His attention span is too short to learn in an academic setting.

This child is switching off his logical brain and has more energy than he can control. The receptive brain is on; however, Charles cannot focus on the lesson the school deems important. Charles may actually be extremely bright, but cannot access his expressive brain in such a way to allow for language skills development.

DOMINANCE PROFILE: Blocked Dominant, Left(language)-brain, left-hand, left-eye, left-ear.

CORRECTION: Cook's Hook-ups, positive points for the teacher, Dennison Laterality Repatterning.

BRAIN GYM: Cook's Hook-ups, cross crawl, thinking cap, brain buttons. It is recommended to expose Charles to dramatic play, gymnastics, and other large motor skill activities.  Blocks, clay, and sand are all excellent activities for Charles. Until he achieves further integration, any emphasis on reading and smaller muscle skills should be avoided.

# TEACHING PERSONAL ECOLOGY
## "Mind over matter; matter over mind."

## WHAT IS PERSONAL ECOLOGY?

No man is an island. We all exist within a physical, energetic, emotional, mental and spiritual ecosystem. What one person does affects everyone else! As teachers who care about the future, we must nourish, not just independence, but interdependence. E-K teaches interdependence. The students who learn to test each other, and who respect the answers they get, learn the highest regard possible for growth and individuality. They also learn gratitude for another human being who takes time and consideration to work with them to support their unique growth.

## SUGGESTED EXPERIMENTS/ EXPERIENCES WITH E-K

### 1. IS STRESS TRANSFERABLE?

Have "Susan" write. Test her looking at her writing. Test other people on the product also. Does stress affect others negatively as well? Does an open flow of energy result in strong muscle tests for others as well?

After Susan is balanced for writing, retest her. She should now be strong. Retest the group, looking at her writing. They should also test strong.

### 2. ARE THOUGHTS TRANSFERABLE?

a. Test a student who is "switched on". Have him or her leave the room. Everyone thinks of something sad in their lives. When he returns retest. Is he affected by the energy in the room? He leaves the room again. Everyone sends a positive thought to him. When he comes back, how is his energy affected?

b. Have "Lisa" think of something stressful, while you test her. Is the muscle "switched off"? Have "Sandy" touch Lisa on the shoulder, while Lisa continues to think about the stressful situation. Test Sandy. Is she also weak? Have "Nathan" touch Sandy on the shoulder. Is Nathan's indicator muscle now affected by Lisa's stressful thoughts, through his physical connection to Sandy? How many students in a chain are affected by Lisa's stress? Will sending her positive thoughts affect the chain? Will holding her Positive Points change the energy for everyone?

c. Have a student turn his back to others. Test the effect on the class.

d. Experiment: Have a student think about something that worries him: a fantasy; e.g., something he already fears or worries about like a car accident, failing school, an earthquake, war, etc. Have him do Cook's Hook-ups or Positive Points. Is it possible to hold onto negative fears or worries in these postures? How long does it take for the energy to disperse? Discuss the implications.

e. Can the individual have a positive effect on his or her environment? Experiment with behavior; e.g., when angry or upset with someone else, do E-K exercises and Cook's Hook-ups. Does the energy in the environment change?

3. FOODS AND OPTIMAL BRAIN POWER

Food is part of our personal ecosystem. Some foods may help us feel and think better; some foods may switch us off and make us feel weak or bad. In E-K, the goal is not to advise a person about what he should or should not eat. Rather, the goal is to teach that food is energy; that some foods have more energy than others; that some energies are more harmonious with our own energy; that some foods deplete us of energy because they deprive us of brain energy by overloading the pancreas and other digestive organs.

There are other considerations about food. These include the amount eaten at one time, the time of day, the level of stress or relaxation while eating, and the environment where one is eating. There are no right and wrong answers when testing foods. Food testing helps us to think about being more aware of our bodies and how we nourish them.

Goals:

a. To teach that food has energy.
b. To teach about the nourishment value in foods.
c. To teach choice making.
d. To teach that emotions and consciousness affect nourishment.

4. FOOD FOR THOUGHT

a. Offer a smorgasbord of possibilities. Some examples: water,
   fruits, vegetables, sprouts, nuts, seeds, candy, sugar, pea-
   nut butter, soft drinks, processed cereals, etc. Test foods
   holding them over the navel. The intention should always
   be, " Is this food nourishing to me?"

b. Test "Andy" holding a food. If he is weak, have "Nick"
   touch his shoulder. Does Andy's potential digestive stress
   affect Nick's energy?

c. Test thinking about foods cooked different ways or in different combinations. Does raw cabbage have the same effect
   as sauerkraut? What about raw eggs, eggs baked in things,
   eggs with cheese, etc. Does a cucumber have the same effect as a pickle? Do baked and raw apples have the same
   effect?

d. Test colors of foods. Are some people more sensitive to
   some colors than others. (We find many gestalt dominant
   people sensitive to foods colored red, orange or pink, like
   strawberries, red wheat, red meat, punch, oranges, etc.)

e. Compare live foods to processed foods; e.g., produce vs.
   something that comes in a box or can. Discuss history of
   food preservation. Discuss food marketing and life expect-
   ancy of food products in different packaging. Test and discuss food additives, by reading labels and testing for different ingredients. If a packaged cereal is weakening, are
   all the ingredients individually weakening also?

f. Test for sugar. If it weakens a person what is the small-
   est amount he can hold and still be weakened? Discuss the

77

amounts of sugar present in cereals, soft drinks, etc. How about hidden sugar found in catsup, salt, spices, mouthwash, frozen canned foods, etc. Did you know that more than a cup of sugar can be in a cup of food? Eg: As a class, research how much sugar is in 1 cup of cola drink. Investigate and discuss the history of sugar., e.g., a medicine for the ancient Egyptians, a source of money and power for slave traders, etc. How much sugar did our grandparents eat, compared to present day? What about sugar cane, is it weakening in its natural form?

g. Can "blessing" or sending good thoughts to food change its negative effect? Can negative thoughts leave a strengthening food with negative energy?

h. Discuss eating habits of different cultures. Discuss foods common in other cultures that are uncommon here in America. How do different students test on these foods?

THE BODY MAKES CHOICES IN ITS ENVIRONMENT

Everything in the environment is a potential energy enhancer or energy robber, just like food and thoughts. There is no end to what you can test.

Everything in the environment can be tested with muscle testing to discover its weakening or strengthening impact on the human being. However, what we teach about "things" and their effects is not as important as what we teach about attitude. This kind of testing has a lasting impact on the belief systems of those we teach. It is said that the Iroquois Indians, before making major decisions, took council to consider the effect of their plans on the next seven generations! As educators and parents, we also must be aware of the far reaching consequences of the attitudes we teach.

"Learn to Choose Life"

In E-K, we are most interested in developing the consciousness of choice. It is not enough to know that something is life enhancing or life depleting. To live in fear of life-negative foods or environments is to trade one evil for another, as the fear itself is a life negating choice. The real key is to develop a large and strong enough sense of Self to choose life. When a person's MFE is 40/40, he is not bothered so much by life-depleting nutritional or environmental factors.

Choose things that tend to jump out at you demanding your attention, as these are usually what affect people the most. Emphasize the positive effects of natural environments, like plants, rocks, and other living things, and soft colors like green and blue, or the natural sounds of water, etc. Emphasize how to use our E-K exercises to keep our energy levels high so we are not negatively effected by things we cannot change.

5. ENVIRONMENTAL FACTORS TO TEST ON:

a. What distance and angle do you test strongest for sitting in front of a TV set?

b. How long can you sit watching TV before getting switched off? What E-K or other exercises switch you on fastest after TV watching?

c. Test on computers, video games and repeat the above tests in #2.

d. Some substances to test: fluorescent lights, cigarette smoke, (an unlit cigarette), alcohol, make-ups, shampoos, colors, aluminum foil, fabrics, perfume and other smells, etc. jewelry (different metals or plastics on different parts of the body), etc. Which are strengthening?

e. Test different types of music. The melody is the music of the "language-expressive" brain. The background beat is the music of the "receptive-reflex" brain. Why does some music

test weak. Test music with an anapestic beat. Does this re-
verse the central meridian? The anapestic beat, two unac-
cented beats followed by an accented one, is opposite to the
heart beat, so it often creates a dichotomy between language
and movement.

f. Discuss energy circuits (e.g., lights, doorbell, etc. and
how to block the circuit or keep it open. Do some environmental substances also block circuits?

g. Test posture: test student sitting, standing, walking, sitting in a chair, holding a pencil and paper, etc. Test different movements of the head and body with "throat open" position (see Switching On for more information) until student
tests strong for all movements.

h. Test reading materials. Test by scanning a page. Test by
just holding a book. Why do some things test strong and
others weak?

We test our students on reading material, assignments, math
problems (have them scan the page), spelling words, etc. We
want them to have lots of "wins", so we encourage them to
stick with what they test strong on. When they test weak on
math problems or spelling words, we know there is a neurological stress and they need some balancing (we use the E-K
dimension tests to locate the area of stress). To study
harder, or to try harder, is simply not the solution, as it
just develops better "abilities" to compensate with switched
off behaviors!

We anchor positive learning with lots of strong muscle
tests, so the student knows he is learning in a way that is
most healthy and beneficial to his whole brain/body system!

6. TESTING FOR "SWITCHED ON" LANGUAGE

Language has an effect on how we feel. Language can be
"switched off". If it lacks gestalt, then it is low on content
or feeling, maybe just a chain of words from the language
brain! If it is an explosive barrage of feeling or emotion
with no logic or control, then it is too gestalt.

Here are some words and phrases on the left (taken from Switching On) that already contain a hidden message. The message is
that "I (or you) am switched off." Compare them to the whole-
brained words on the right.

| | |
|---|---|
| "Try" | "I do my best" |
| "Stretch" | "Reach" or "Lengthen" |
| "I hope" | "I plan" or "I trust" |
| "I want" | "I will" |
| "I can't remember" | "I didn't remember yet" |
| "I lost" | "I didn't win this time" |
| "I stopped" | "I didn't finish yet" |
| "I quit" | "I'm taking a break" |
| "I have a problem" | "I meet challenges" |
| "I hate..." | "I prefer...something else." |
| "You never..." | "Let's..." |
| "I'm sorry" | "I'll fix it...""How can I help?" |

Discuss hidden messages in language that insist on finding
blame. What alternatives are there? Do you really mean it
when you say, "She broke the plate," or isn't it only true that
"The plate broke "?


Our language is replete with expressions, like the following,
which are loaded with energy which stresses and weakens us.

He broke her heart.
She spoiled that child.
That knocks me out.
That makes me sick.
He's a pain in the neck.
They ought to be shot.
He'll have to take me the way I am!
I can't get over it.
I could just die.
I'm going broke.
There's no end to this mess!
This is killing me.

What's the matter with me?
I'm killing time.
Everything depends on me!
I'm no good.
I can't think straight.
Just this one time won't hurt anything.
You can't do that - better let me.
You'll catch your death of cold.
You're going to break your neck.
Oh, that's nothing.  Wait until you hear what happened to me.

Encourage the children to monitor their own language and to
change it consciously to have a more positive energy.  Notice,
over time, that the class develops a higher morale and that
stress levels improve as the hidden, switched off, energy in
language is transmuted to positive, switched on, language.

# TIPS FOR INTEGRATED LEARNING IN THE CLASSROOM
## "Creating the now moment"

After students are "switched on", whole-brain learning experiences like these are more effective.

## MOVEMENT BREAKS

Take short "Movement breaks" often: Raise the energy of the group with 10 minutes of cross crawl, dance, figure 8's, lenthening exercises, hand-eye coordination games with a soft ball, etc. Use high energy classical music or waltzes to center the group. Modern children's music like that of Marcia Berman, Hap Palmer, or Ella Jenkins, as well as music of other cultures, helps to shift energy.

## ALTERNATE ACTIVITIES

Alternate "receptive" skills with "expressive" skills", for example:

| "Receptive" | "Expressive" |
|---|---|
| Reading | talking/discussing |
| Listening | writing |
| sitting | whole body movement |
| copying | free form drawing |
| paperwork (math, | kinesthetic work (beads, |
| writing, etc.) | blocks, rods, etc.) |
| repetitive tasks | free form writing |
| T/F or multiple | Essay tests |
| choice tests | |

## WRITING OUT BREAKS

This whole-brain exercise helps to improve clarity of writing and thinking by clearing out "language debris" from the surface of the mind. Give students a short period occasionally, about 10-20 minutes, in which the instructions are to "write as much as you can about anything which comes to mind." When they are finished they must destroy the paper and throw it away.

"DRAWING OUT"

In this exercise, the person "focuses on a particular feeling (eg: anger, fear, joy, sadness, pain) and "draws it out" of her mind and body with the use of paper and pencil, crayon, scissors, colored tissue, clay, etc. This is a non-judgemental activity, and the product may be disposed of without analysis.

EXPRESSIVE BREAKS
("Expressive Breaks" activate the back/front dimension.)

Expressive Oral Language:

1. Group discussions about personal feelings. Students sit in Cooks-Hook-ups and express how they feel.

2. Creative endings or possibilities are discussed for a story, a view of history, or a newspaper article the class has read. How do the alternatives we choose reflect our beliefs about life? How could these alternatives change the future? Can our beliefs about the past change? What factors are constant?

4. A group story is developed, each person volunteering with his own segment or idea. This helps to develop the common integration area of the brain by bringing together personal experience with other information and turning it into self-generating language.

5. History and culture: play the music or dances of different cultures and historical times and discuss what the people must be like and how they might feel.

Expressive Written Language:

1. Students write and/or draw short stories about themselves. Build a notebook of thoughts over a period of time.

2. Use these "notebooks" for oral reading time, giving the child space to fill in or alter his previous thoughts through his own verbal experimentation.

3. Write poetry or prose. Make available a list of one or two syllable rhyming words. Talk about interesting phonetic sounds. Start with any short, intriguing sentence. Note the rhythm of the syllables. Play with the rhythms and sounds of language.

# ART ON THE MIDLINE
## "Kinesthetics esthetics"

These bi-hemispheric drawings are easy and fun. Once children discover their abilities to produce them without supervision, they
love exploring the space on the paper with both hands at once!

These exercises encourage fine motor skills and eye/hand coordination. They encourage the ability to keep both eyes and both brain
hemispheres "switched on" crossing the midline in a fluid way.

These exercises should be done with materials (chalk, crayons, pen-
cils) which are comfortable to use and hold with either hand. No
judgement should ever be made, good or bad, regarding the ability
of one hand over the other. Be it understood that the more experienced hand will be easier to control in the beginning. When the
student does these drawings, he must always sit or stand on the
midline point of his visual-writing field.

1. Begin with figure 8's for the eyes, large figure 8's on the
   chalkboard, using one hand, then the other, then both together.

2. Let the child explore 2-handed space on the chalkboard, drawing
   free form. Encourage the use of both hands at the same time.

3. Draw waves with the child as in figure 1., then explore variations of the circle, as in figure 2. Encourage other symmetrical figures such as rectangles, triangles, and diamonds.

4. Introduce free-form bi-lateral patterns and line drawings of
   symmetrical objects of his own choice such as vases, faces,
   trees, etc.

5. Introduce mirror writing with both hands as a game. Some children are quite adept at this and are fascinated by the look and
   feel of this skill.

As the child experiences the joy of using his non-writing hand, and begins to have more control over it, he will explore designs of his own choosing. Both children and adults with whom we work discover that they are immediately able to draw in a more fluid, less judgmental way.

Children love the element of surprise that is built into this form of art. Drawing becomes more fun as shapes and images appear from the unconscious. As the gestalt brain switches on, space, shadow and form become more apparent. Movement of the hands becomes more automatic and relaxed, coming from the whole arms and shoulders.

Older children often find they are soon able to master mirror writing. This increases their skill at visualization and memory, as well as eye-hand coordination. The integrated ability to analyze shape and form and to sense the whole at the same time is a delightful experience.

Do we ever encourage a child to change her writing hand? Never. If it is appropriate for a child to change hands, it would happen automatically, as she became more integrated. However, when both brain hemispheres are on, whichever hand the child already uses will become the perfect tool for her near-point expression.

**1.**

**2.**

**3.**

NAME_____

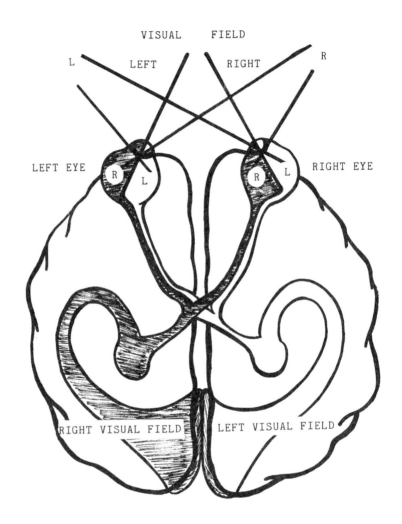

VISUAL   FIELD

COLOR IN YOUR DOMINANT (FOCUSING) EYE.

TESTED WITH E-K ON_____

# MY DOMINANT EAR

NAME_____

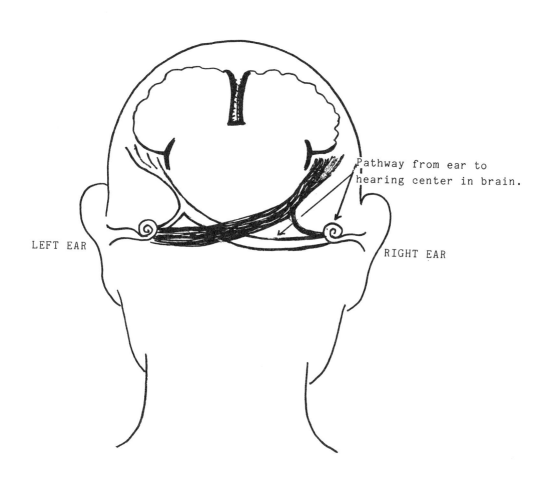

Pathway from ear to
hearing center in brain.

LEFT EAR

RIGHT EAR

COLOR IN YOUR DOMINANT EAR.  (COLOR BOTH IF TESTED AS BALANCED).

ESTED WITH E-K ON_____

93

NAME_____

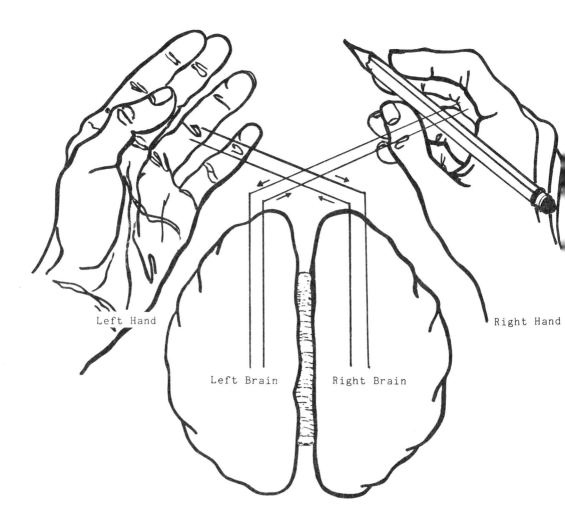

Left Hand                                                    Right Hand

Left Brain          Right Brain

Color in your dominant brain and dominant hand
(color both hands if you are ambidexterous).

TESTED WITH E-K ON_____

NAME_____

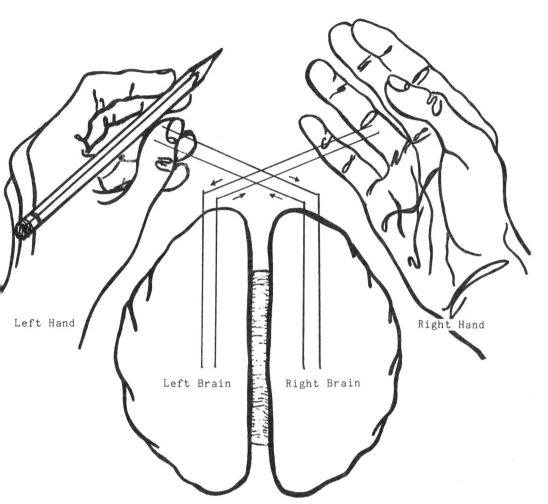

Left Hand

Right Hand

Left Brain

Right Brain

Color in your dominant brain and dominant hand
(color both hands if you are ambidexterous).

TESTED WITH E-K ON_____

NAME_____

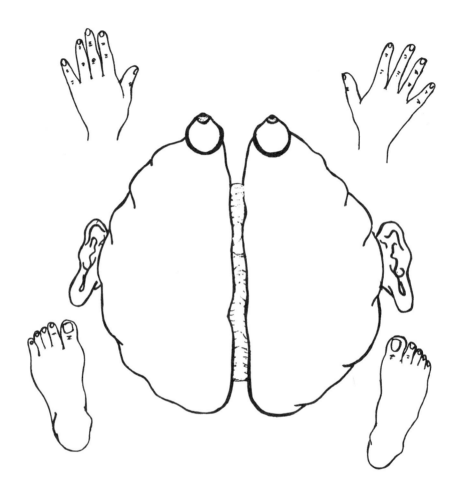

My LANGUAGE HEMISPHERE helps me to think and act consciously, speak, listen, read lines, write, be aware of time, and many other things.

My GESTALT HEMISPHERE helps me to visualize, sense space, coordinate movement, imagine, relax, experience feelings and emotions, and much more.

TOGETHER, THEY MAKE A GREAT TEAM!  PLENTY OF LOVING COMMUNICATION, PLAY, TOUCHING, EXERCISE, GOOD FOOD AND MUSIC, AND INTERESTING BOOKS AND IDEAS WILL NOURISH BOTH SIDES AND HELP THEM TO WORK TOGETHER VERY HAPPILY!

COLOR IN YOUR DOMINANCE PATTERN          TESTED WITH E-K ON_____

# DEFINITION OF TERMS

**ANALYTIC** — Refers to the ability to perceive reality as isolated, separate parts without attention to their context as a whole.

**BLENDING** — The synthesis of separate parts, such as phonetic speech sounds, into longer, more meaningful, wholes.

**COMPENSATORY APPROACH** — The approach to education for learning disabilities which emphasizes that children must accept their situation and learn to adjust to it by maximizing a strength and compensating for any weaknesses.

**CROSS DOMINANCE** — The inherited predisposition to be dominant with one hand, usually the right, and dominant with the alternate eye and/or ear at the same time.

**DECODE** — The analysis of any symbolic language into a meaningful message.

**DOMINANCE** — The inherited preference for one cerebral hemisphere over the other for handedness, eyedness, earedness, etc.

**DYSLEXIA** — The inability to decode the printed symbol due to the inhibition of the receptive centers of the brain. Broadly, any learning disability which causes confusion and requires compensatory behaviors.

**ECHO-EFFECT** — The memory of the spoken symbol by sound alone, without attention to meaningful clues.

**EDUCATIONAL KINESIOLOGY** — The study of the musculature system of the body and its relationship to whole brain learning.

**EDU-KINESTHETICS** — The application of kinesthetics (movement) to the study of right brain, left brain, and body integration for purposes of eliminating stress and maximizing full learning potential.

**ENCODE** — The expression of meaning and language through the use of written symbols.

**FEEDBACK** — That short term memory skill which enables one to hear his own voice repeating what he has thought, read, or heard.

**FEEDFORWARD** — That short term memory skill which enables one to anticipate his own voice speaking something from long term memory.

**GESTALT** — The ability to perceive reality as a whole or totality without attention to analysis of its separate parts.

**HOMOLATERAL** - The involuntary choice to access only one cerebral hemisphere at any given moment, thus blocking integrated thought and movement.

97

**IMPULSE** — The intuitive reponse to a situation, without mediation through language or analytical thought.

**INTEGRATION** — The life long process of realizing one's physical, mental, and spiritual potential, the first step being the simultaneous activation of both cerebral hemispheres as described in this book.

**MIDFIELD** — The area where one visual and hemispheric field overlaps the other for integrated learning.

**MIDLINE** — The line which separates one visual field and hemispheric awareness from the other when there is incomplete integration.

**MUSCLE TESTING** — In **E-K**, used for two purposes. **1.** To measure the relative strength of a muscle for the purpose of infering brain functions relevant to educators. **2.** To anchor or to reinforce positively all integrated processing.

**"REFLEX"** — To act without conscious thought and with self-preservation as the primary motivation. Used as a verb in **E-K** to suggest the movements initiated by the gestalt brain when one is homolateral and not yet integrated.

**"REVERSED"** — The involuntary inhibition of the language brain, due to some negativity, often resulting in movement preferred from right to left as opposed to left to right, causing reading reversals.

**SIMULTANEOUS PROCESSING** — That ability to access both cerebral hemispheres at one and the same time, maximizing hemispheric integration and reducing stressful learning.

**"SWITCHED OFF"** — The involuntary inhibition of one cerebral hemisphere in order to better access the other, due to stress or lack of integration.

**SYNCHRONICITY** — The state of harmony in the universe where everything fits and flows together without stress. This state of consciousness begins with hemispheric integration.

**"TRANSPOSED"** — The inherited, neurological organization of the brain, whereby the language, speech centers are located in the right cerebral hemisphere instead of the left where they are found in 85% of the population.

# ABOUT THE AUTHORS

**Paul E. Dennison, Ph.D.,** has been an educator for all of his professional life. He is the creator of the Edu-Kinesthetics and Brain Gym processes, and a pioneer in applied brain research. His discoveries are based upon an understanding of the interdependence of physical development, language acquisition, and academic achievement. This perspective grew out of his background in curriculum development and experimental psychology at the University of Southern California, where he was granted a Doctorate in Education for his research in beginning reading achievement and its relationship to thinking. For nineteen years, Dr. Dennison served as director of the Valley Remedial Group Learning Centers in Southern California, helping children and adults turn their difficulties into successful growth. He is the author of twelve books and manuals, including *Switching On: A Guide to Edu-Kinesthetics.*

**Gail E. Dennison** is the co-author with her husband, Dr. Dennison, of the Edu-Kinesthetics series of books and manuals. The simple illustrations in the Edu-K books speak of her love of children and movement. As a dancer, she has brought grace and focus to the Brain Gym® activities. Gail has a varied background in the teaching of brain integration, including ten years' experience as a Touch for Health instructor. Gail's interest in perception and developmental skills comes through in the Edu-K vision courses. She developed the *Visioncircles* course and the *Vision Gym™* movements, in which rhythm, color, and form provide the basis for experiences that offer visual and perceptual growth. Gail is the creator of the *Brain Gym Journal,* and heads the publication committee for the Educational Kinesiology Foundation.

The following are some of the courses offered by the Educational Kinesiology Foundation, 1575 Spinnaker Drive, Suite 204B, Ventura, CA 93001 • (800) 356-2109 • www.braingym.org

## BASIC-LEVEL COURSES

★ **BRAIN GYM®** – 24 hours, consisting of Part I, **The Lateral Brain** and Part II, **The Whole Brain**
This Brain Gym course offers an in-depth experience of hemispheric integration through Dennison Laterality Repatterning and 23 Brain Gym activities that relate to whole-brain functioning. A process for achieving deeper structural integration through Three-Dimension Repatterning is also included. The effects of incomplete development of laterality, centering, and focus on posture, reading, writing, spelling, and memory are identified and balanced. Course Manual: *Brain Gym® Handbook* by Dennison and Dennison.

★ **VISIONCIRCLES** – 24 hours
The Visioncircles course provides a road map to completion of developmental skills through movement, play, and art. It offers vision enhancement through activities that nourish perceptual flexibility. Each of the eight structured sessions embodies a unique perceptual slant and emphasizes different visual and kinesthetic skills. Participants learn 34 Vision Gym movements for integrating visual, auditory, and tactile abilities. Course Manual: *The Visioncircles Handbook.* Prerequisites: Brain Gym, Parts I & II.

## PROFESSIONAL-LEVEL COURSES

★ **EDUCATIONAL KINESIOLOGY IN-DEPTH: The Seven Dimensions of Intelligence** — 32 hours
Learn and practice the Educational Kinesiology principles through an individualized educational model. Receive hands-on experience with seven dimensions of body movement, focusing on how each can support or block the learning process. Other areas covered in the course include: appropriate goal setting, learning theory, and growth-oriented communication. Course Manual: *Educational Kinesiology In Depth: The Seven Dimensions of Intelligence.* Prerequisites include: Brain Gym, Parts I & II.

★ **BRAIN GYM TEACHER PRACTICUM** — 32 hours
A certification course qualifying the student to teach Brain Gym. Completion of this California state-approved course provides the graduate with specific skills for teaching the Brain Gym course. This workshop prepares the instructor to represent the Foundation in the community as a member of its staff. Course Manual: *Teacher Practicum Manual.* Prerequisites include: *Educational Kinesiology In Depth.*

# EDU-KINESTHETICS, INC. PUBLICATIONS

**U.S. Funds**

**SWITCHING ON** by Dr. Paul E. Dennison ...........................................................$15.95

**EDU-K FOR KIDS** by Dennison & Dennison ......................................................$15.95

**PERSONALIZED WHOLE BRAIN INTEGRATION** by Dennison & Dennison ....$17.95

**BRAIN GYM® TEACHERS EDITION** by Dennison & Dennison ..........................$16.95

**BRAIN GYM® FOR BUSINESS** by Dennison & Dennison & Teplitz ..................$12.95

**EDUCATIONAL KINESIOLOGY IN DEPTH**........................................................$29.95

**INTEGRATED MOVEMENTS** (audio tape) ..........................................................$12.00

Prices subject to change without notice.

Mail your order to:
**Edu-Kinesthetics, Inc.,** Post Office Box 3395. Ventura, California 93006-3395 U.S.A.
Telephone or Fax Ordering with VISA/MC:
Telephone (805) 650-3303 or Toll Free (888) 388-9898 • FAX (805) 650-1689
Visit us on the Web at: www.braingym.com

Prices do not include postage and handling charges. Please add $3.95 (US) for shipping for single title orders. For orders of multiple titles: Please add $3.95 (US) for the first title and 75 cents (US) for each additional title. California residents must add sales tax. Quantity discounts available. Allow three weeks delivery time.